Discourses
Volume Two
2015

DISCOURSES:
Re-Union of Soul and Spirit
Volume Two: 2015

Yogacharya David R. Hickenbottom

Editor: Ruth M. Lamb, Ph.D

The Cross and The Lotus Publishing
Camano Island, Washington, USA

For permission requests, contact the publisher at:
http://www.crossandlotus.com/contact.html

ISBN: 978-1-957811-00-0 (softcover)
ISBN: 978-1-957811-99-4 (eBook)

All photos courtesy of Carla Hickenbottom Portfolio
unless otherwise attributed (see page 205)

Edited by Ruth Lamb

Book design by Jan Westendorp/Kato Design and Photo (katodesignandphoto.com)

Cover design by Rob Landers, Ruth Lamb, and Jan Westendorp

Printed and bound in the USA

Published by
The Cross and The Lotus Publishing
Camano Island, Washington, USA
Website: www.crossandlotus.com

Contents

OM TAT SAT AUM

Preface

Yogacharya David, Puri, India, 2013.

Re-union of soul and Spirit, after so long living in the Great Divorce from God, is the theme for this life-time. . . . To find the real resolution from suffering is the work we are here to do.

The key to gaining spiritual freedom . . . is the ability to learn from our experience. This ability to learn from experience is basic to all growth. So many people repeat the same errors and expect different results: this is insanity. The soul who wishes to really grow must be a keen observer of cause and effect, for this is the universal law of creation.

How can we remain in a shadow existence when that is not who we are? Realize that there is much more to us. Let us demand our birthright, proclaim our freedom, and manifest all that we are in truth. This is the task for which we have come and it waits for us to step into the Divine Image and Likeness of who and what we truly are.

—Yogacharya David

A time can come in our individual evolution when our soul turns to eternal things—the soul seeks a deeper understanding of suffering and its resultant loss of caring, loss of kindness, loss of compassion, loss of honesty, and foremost, a loss of love—with this loss, the human spirit becomes depleted. Societies disintegrate; great cultures collapse; wars and strife find room to grow, and people themselves find little joy in living and turn to solace in depression, anxiety, addiction, or anger and greed, or a multiple of other thieves-of-the-spirit attractions. Contact with love, bliss, joy, and helpful, hopeful, creativity is lost; the mask of death seems to cover all goodness—death seems to govern.

Darkness descends on humankind and this beautiful planet—until the courageous reawaken their wisdom—until the soul-force reactivates through aspiration for Light, Truth, and Love, and again reignites the spirit within.

The ancient Vedic saying, "By Truth is the progress towards Truth," needs to be grasped once more by striving souls, then the law of truth can again come forth from the great universal source of superconscious Truth.

If you have been asking: Why am I here? What is my purpose? Especially now, as the world tumbles into uncertainty and ragged leadership, with individual and national sovereignty hanging by a thread, you will find that Yogacharya David's *Re-Union of Soul and*

Spirit discourses can provide you not only with solace, but also with a sure guidance that you can apply in your own unique way—in a manner that suits where your life path is at this moment.

In *Re-Union of Soul and Spirit*, Yogacharya David shares his own struggle: his pain, his joy, and his faith—he also shares the amazing synchronicities that come with pure intention and a willingness to listen deeply to his highest wisdom and spirit's promptings. He encourages the God-seed within to stretch his consciousness toward the Light of God—Universal Spirit—Universal Divinity, the greatest un-nameable Source of all that is.

We can, in our 21st Century design, follow our earlier spiritual elders—spiritual scientists—and learn again how to enter the inner sanctuaries of our soul and rediscover the indwelling Light of the universe: Yogacharya David provides accessible guidance.

In a series of six volumes of Discourses, Yogacharya David blesses us with his gathering wisdom, his deep understanding of the perilous nature of a climb that can take us to the highest spiritual summits, and the joy that comes from attunement with Spirit, as we learn how to reunite soul and spirit so that we can reawaken to who we truly are and reclaim our life-purpose. Let us join Yogacharya David and climb!

The volumes are as follows:

- *Discourses—Volume One: 2013–14: Living a Spiritually Rich Life*

- *Discourses—Volume Two: 2015: Re-Union of Soul and Spirit*

- *Discourses—Volume Three: 2016: A True New Birth*

- *Discourses—Volume Four: 2017: Gateway to the Infinite*

- *Discourses—Volume Five: 2018: Standing on the Threshold of Eternity*

- *Discourses—Volume Six: 2019: Writing in the Book of Life*

Regarding the use of images in this publication:

Yogacharya David put great care, creativity, time, and intention into selecting images to complement his writings in each and every posting. When preparing his Discourses for publication, we found that certain images from unknown sources, or those which were found to be under copyright, could not be included. Every effort has been made to feature replacement images as close as possible to Yogacharya David's original selections. In a few instances, where no similar substitute was available, a picture of Yogacharya David or a beloved saint has been offered instead.[1] Substitute images are designated in the caption by a double asterisk **. For example: Yogacharya David at Anandashram, 2005.** Image attribution is in the Reference section of the book.

OM TAT SAT AUM

---

[1] Yogacharya David's original discourses can be found at **www.crossandlotus.com**

Introduction

Yogacharya David, Haridwar, India, 2005.

Dear Aspirant,

Whenever you begin a journey, you usually start with a destination in mind, a means of conveyance, and a map or landmarks to indicate that you are on the right path. Those of us following this path have God (Self) Realization as our Goal of goals. Our means of conveyance is God-remembrance, such as chanting God's Name, deepened meditation through Kriya Yoga, universal love and service, loving God, and discernment of Truth.

These writings often come in the early morning: a time when the day is quiet and fresh, an open page upon which to write. These thought-expressions come from an unfathomable Source, welling up from the quiet of the all-pervading Spirit. Reading these words has the power to lead you to the same Source from which they have flowed from within me.

The inspiration that fuels these writings comes to me with great power and clarity; however, mere words are incapable of holding all that is given. It is through inner attunement that the power in the words will lift you into the same Spirit that I experience in super-consciousness, an uplifting power that is a passageway into realms divine.

Human words and thought are imperfect; it is only in pure Spirit that perfection is to be truly found. It is the purpose of these writings that we should rise together in the universal Spirit of God. Come, let us soar together and find truth and beauty unencumbered.

These discourses can act as markers upon your spiritual journey to make for safe and rapid progress. Unlike a scattered "hunt and peck" approach chosen by many taking them on "wild goose chases" only to become thoroughly lost, you will receive teachings of the purest quality that speed you on the most direct path to realization. Obstacles arise that create challenges for your journey—you can find inspiration here to help you meet those challenges.

These writings contain notes from pilgrimages and journeys which also (reader alert here!) have lessons upon the path embedded in them.[2]

With deepest love and blessings on your journey,
YOGACHARYA DAVID

---

2   Much of this Introduction comes from Yogacharya David's Discourses, *Volume One - 2013–14: Living a Spiritually Rich Life.*

DISCOURSES

January 1

A HAPPY HANGOVER

Paramhansa Yogananda,
The Last Smile, 1952.**

New Year's was brought in in the same manner that I have celebrated for the past 35 years, with a Meditation Service. Mother Hamilton was doing this each year when I met her. I remember these times. When nearing midnight, we could hear firecrackers going off in the neighborhood, Mother would wish us, "Happy New Year."

Many people are used to "celebrating" in alternate ways, many times drinking too much, *trying* to have a good time, and many are feeling lonely and unhappy. Far too many wake up in the morning with some kind of hangover that makes them feel very bad.

Last night we watched a talk of Mother's and listened to Yogananda speak. I felt the uplifting power in the room and the purity of Spirit as we "dumped our minds into super-consciousness" and soared "with wings as eagles."

Well into the early morning that beautiful Spirit sang its song throughout every cell of my Being. The feeling of completeness, wholeness, and perfection was with me, and so too with many who joined our Service in person, through Ustream and in Spirit.

And this morning, the song of Aum, and the qualities of purity, love, and gratitude continue to thrill my soul, like listening to the most sublime symphony echoing through all eternity. Oh, what joy is mine! I remember back to early years, my vain pursuit of happiness in the worldly way, that even at the time felt hollow. Tears of gratitude pour out of me, "Oh Lord, my cup runs over with the wine of Your Bliss, my heart melts and runs like a river of love, and You make me know that we are ever united in the ocean of mirth."

This is my kind of "hangover."

January 5

YOUR TRUE LIKENESS AND IMAGE

Garuda: Vishnu's Eagle-God at Puri.

For many of us, the busy time of the holidays is over. The annual holy-days of Thanksgiving, Christmas, and the birth of a New Year are passed. For most, these times will create new memories of love, family, and sacred moments.

Because this is such a powerful time of year, others will feel the pang of pain due to loved ones who are no longer present and losses of various kinds. The keen remembrance of loss reminds us that there is only one constant in all creation, and that is our loving Creator—the Father and Mother of all that exists.

The recurring healing message is that by attunement with heavenly Father and Divine Mother, all wounds, hurts, and losses may be soothed with the salve of growing peace, joy, and love.

This re-union of soul and Spirit, after so long living in the Great Divorce from God, is the theme for this lifetime. All great myths, stories, and scriptures expressed throughout the world, and down through all time, come to one central point: to find the resolution from suffering; this is the real work we are here to do.

The key to gaining spiritual freedom, that is the removal of suffering, is the ability to learn from our experience. This ability to learn from experience is basic to all growth. So many people repeat the same errors and expect different results: this is insanity. The soul who wishes to really grow must be a keen observer of cause and effect, for this is the universal law of creation.

As we eye this new year, let us not simply list those things we wish to change, as we have listed in previous years. Create a solid plan with behavioral benchmarks. Be determined to apply the spiritual principles we have been taught and let us become master of ourselves. Do not allow another year to go by treading water only, when we are meant to soar in the skies!

Let our eagle heart rise to the heavens and know ourselves to be spiritual dynamos who can remove mountains of suffering for ourselves and for others. We are made in the image and likeness of the Infinite Being; this is the Truth!

How can we remain in a shadow existence when that is not who we are? Realize there is so much more to us. Let us demand our birthright, proclaim our freedom, and manifest all that we are in truth. This is the task for which we have come, and it waits for us to step into the Divine Image and Likeness of who, and what, we truly are.

January 12

OH, THE PLACES YOU'LL GO!

Yogacharya David, on a hike in
Glacier National Park, Montana.**

In a current survey of spiritual literature, there is a broad spectrum of attitudes about God, the ultimate Reality, and the world we live in. There are examples of those who give up everything in this world, even a loin cloth, to overcome the limiting pull of worldly attraction in order to know God. Then there are others who seem to be book and retreat "production machines" who are apparently making millions by writing and talking about "spiritual" living.

What are we to believe about realizing God and our relationship to this world? In our Kriya lineage we read the most interesting account of Babaji manifesting a palace for Lahiri Mahasaya in order to satisfy a latent desire. And Swami Ramdas writes that the "World Is God." And yet we know that attachment to this world is a major stumbling block on the road to realization.

We must make a careful analysis to perceive the truth of the matter; this is especially true given how deceptive the ego-mind is. On our journey to realization, we know that things of the world definitely bring the mind down from inner states of peace and bliss. This battle between the uplifting forces and downward attractions is tremendous.

But not everything in this world is a temptation. What will be a great attraction for one person may have no appeal to another. Therefore, the object of attraction is not the problem, it is the attachment the mind forms for a person, place, or thing.

A good rule of thumb is that when you feel the pull of strong attraction, avoid it. Instead, place your mind firmly upon God until the "fever" of attraction has completely passed. Even then, be very careful not to provoke an attraction by becoming too familiar with it; for slumbering embers can too easily awaken into burning passions.

God has taken me through many experiences in my relationship with this world. He gradually took everything away from me in the worldly sense; finally, He took job and profession as well. When I spent a year in silence and seclusion, I had but a few items of furniture: a meditation chair, a table, and a mat for a bed.

After having taken me out of this world, Divine Will seemed intent on bringing me back into it. First came marriage, that came with a dowry of a Ford Escort car and a few more items of furniture. Then, through His good graces, we lived with others from place to place, then rented a house, then we bought a house, more cars came our way, and this last year another house! Just this week, He has brought us to California where we are staying in my brother's beautiful motor home for three weeks in a magnificent RV park in Palm Desert.

As we sit surrounded by motor homes, some of them costing over a million dollars, the question comes, "What is my relationship to all of this?" Ever since my year in silence, I have been established in an immovable stillness within. Somehow, whatever comes does not touch this stillness that directly merges with the great, supreme Reality. These gifts of material things are God's play, His lila. If ever I notice that the Still-Presence is disturbed by these outer happenings, I will instantly run away.

Even with this inner detachment, I feel that I should be a good steward of what has been given. Cars and house should be kept in good working order, uplifting beauty created, and an open hand is kept for giving to others what has been given to me as God directs.

This abundance that has come is a logic-defying play that unfolds before my astounded vision. I say "logic-defying" because with having renounced all, so much has now come; it really goes against what the worldly mind would think. However, even with this material prosperity, what is profoundly clear to me is that happiness begins within. If every material thing was suddenly gone and all I had was God, I truly know that in Him I have everything!

Perhaps even those authors who have made millions also have God, for all things are possible with Him. But it is rare for someone with millions to know that God is the source of all prosperity, not a bank account or a portfolio.

Remaining steady in the face of life's ups and downs brings to mind my favorite Dr. Seuss book (in truth the only one of his I have read), "Oh, The Places You'll Go!" In this story our intrepid traveler (you) goes through all the ups and the terrifying downs, but ever proceeds upon his or her way; a parable of life's journey.

This life does take you to so many places, in body, mind, and spirit; every one of them has great meaning in your ultimate adventure in going to God. The key to finding happiness in the journey is to find that place of stillness within your heart and soul, and never let it go. Then be in wonder as God unfolds His life within you and all around you; and oh, the places you will go!

> Congratulations!
>
> Today is your day.
>
> Your off to Great Places!
>
> Your off and away!
>
> You have brains in your head.
>
> You have feet in your shoes.
>
> You can steer yourself
>
> any direction you choose.
>
> —DR. SEUSS[3]

---

3   Dr. Seuss. www.goodreads.com

January 13

CARLA, HAPPY BIRTHDAY!

Carla Hickenbottom, Happy Birthday!

Today marks the day Carla was born to this world for this present incarnation. Astrologers tell us there is significance to the exact moment of birth. I can only say that I have noticed that I always had very good days on the much-maligned Friday the 13th, and on just such a day Carla was born.

Because Carla's nature is to quietly serve, I wanted you to know just a few things about her that I find noteworthy. From the very beginning, Carla would make comments on something she heard in a talk of Mother's or mine, and how she had been thinking about it for the week, putting it to work in her life. So many hear a talk and get a great upliftment from it, but taking a theme and staying with it all week, or longer, is really something to admire.

As I say, Carla serves quietly in the background. From the wedding day forward, powerful spiritual forces have been at work in her. We immediately embarked for Anandashram, and it was there that Carla began the Mystical Crucifixion. The Kundalini force rose powerfully through her spine, creating great internal heat. She was "nailed" upon her cross, her body, with "thieves" on either side, one pulling her up, and the other triggering every dark fear and mood. She went to the Bible to look for the truth behind the words. Through it all, she never turned away from the Light or what God asked her to do.

To this day, powerful forces are at work in her. It can make her service to me and others a great challenge at times, but she strives always to do all she can. If anything, these internal experiences make her nature even more indrawn; it is easy to see why yogis look for isolated retreats in order to deepen their communion with God. But it brings balance to our lives to be in joyful seva, service. And Carla serves so willingly, wanting to bring the teachings to one and all, to create beauty in this world, to so serve as to make Mother say, "Well done!"

So, these are just a few notes, to "lift the veil" and reveal a bit of the extraordinary Soul residing in her current form. It always gives me such joy when others recognize, as many do, those great qualities that run in those still waters.

Carla, from all of us, Happy Birthday!

January 18

FROM THE GECKO TO THE LADY IN FLUORESCENT PINK SHOES

Palm Canyon palm trees.

God is equally present everywhere: thus affirms the great scriptures of the world and realized Beings down through time. And so God proves on a daily basis as He has taken us hither and yon. We have traveled to the deserts of Southern California to be here with devotees and to see how Divine Mother manifests Herself in this part of the world. Mother thought this the most wonderful place 55 years ago, and it still is.

We have motored our way to Borrego Springs where Rick and Judy have their RV parked in the desert, "boon-docking" in the midst of purple and brown shaded mountains. Rajasi Janakananda (James J. Lynn), Dr. Lewis, and Bob Raymer, all had homes in this area, using them as retreats. Mother came here after returning from India in 1958 during her recovery from paralysis suffered during her Mystical Crucifixion.

It is easy to see why they found this area conducive to healing and raising consciousness. There is such a pure and expansive feeling in this desert. Indeed, saints have sought out the desert from time immemorial in order to find solitude and pure vibration. Perhaps we will be brought back some day in order to spend more time here.

From the simplicity of boon-docking, we return to the glamor of Palm Desert—El Paseo is a "tony" shopping area that would please more discriminating buyers. With beautifully lit boulevards that are banked on either side by walled off golf courses, deluxe hotels, and resorts, it is simply amazing how water changes brown hills to green grass and rising palms trees. Bread may be the staff of life, but water is the absolutely essential ingredient for all life on this planet.

And God is pulsating Life through it all. From the lonely gecko sunning on a rock to the pink shod lady walking her purebred pooch past brand name stores, it is all Divine Mother parading Her life in a variety that is dizzying in its multiplicity. To the unbiased eye, both manifest a singular mystery and beauty that pulse with bliss. Is the life in the water flowing up the center of the palm tree not the same as what manifests in the lady in fluorescent pink shoes? And is not all life from the same Source, and a blissful expression of God?

Through pure vision, the kingdom of Heaven is seen spread all over this earth, and with eyes to see, and ears to hear, it is unallayed joy to behold it. May you also know that kingdom as it manifests in your life, and that you can feel His bliss, now and always.

January 23

THE NEEDLE AND THE MAGNET

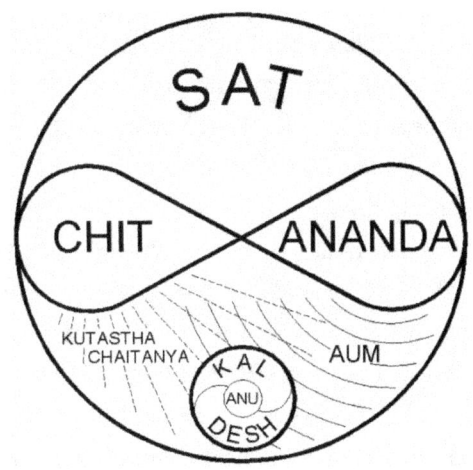

Sat Chit Ananda, drawing by Reverend Larry Koler.

Based on Sri Yukteswar's writings, Sat Chit Ananda are the eternal qualities of God: Being, Consciousness, and Bliss. From the Light of God, Kutastha Chaitanya (Christ Consciousness), and the sound-vibration of Aum (Amen), manifest Kal (time), Desh (space), and Anu (particle/atoms that make up material creation).

It is thrilling to get updates from aspirants describing the spiritual work they are doing, and especially so when some special insight or vision is had that brings resolution to a long-term problem, doubt, or question. I thought I would include this email I received from Charmie that closely reflects a vision God had once given to me (this is used with permission and with minor edits). The reasoning mind is simply not big enough to get answers to some questions; only through intuition (in this case a Superconscious dream) can we get a glimpse into the gigantic dimensions of this creation and how it really is His play, and that it really is perfect.

Dear David,

During our Bellingham Service on Wednesday, we listened to the talk you gave at Rick and Judy's. What a surprise to hear the title, *The Needle and the Magnet*. Because, last Friday night I had a dream, one of those wonderful "real" dreams.

Let me preface this, I have been having a conversation with God about the state of the world: the wars, and starvation, and hatred, etc. I told Him that I understand He has a plan, but it seems so chaotic and ugly from here. And this was His response, it came to me in the best way for me, when I am "unconscious to the world," i.e., sleeping.

I saw the universe black, with swirling lights and movement all around. Then I went further out, to the non-universe (?), and I watched the black movement. I saw there was a center, not a black center, but a Golden Light Center—it was definitely a magnet. All of the universe created a pattern, it was the same as you see when you lay a magnet in the middle of iron filings. In this case the "filings" were actually moving. We are all those iron filings, and God is the Magnet; not only individual people, but the planets, the stars, the empty space—all. We were going toward God on the one end, and then being propelled away from God at the other end, and the loop kept going. We were drawn to the Center, then propelled out into seeming chaos, and as it came back in toward God, it became more orderly and narrow. The funny thing was that when the one section (Was it a universe?) was going in, another was going out. It was a beautiful dance of little iron filings around the Center. And the chaos helped to create the dance as much as the orderly parts.

Do I understand this with my mind? No. Does my heart and soul understand and see the beauty? Yes.

I just had to share this because of your talk about magnetism.

Thank you for Being David, and for Serving.

Om Sri Ram Jai Ram Jai Jai Ram—Victory!

January 26

THEORY FOR LASTING HAPPINESS

Mother Hamilton, India, 1968.**

We all have theories about how this world works. Many people carry on their "programs" for seeking happiness with little analysis of what actually does or does not work. A life unexamined is bound to repeat errors ad infinitum until there is some regard for learning from experience.

The ability to observe and learn from experience is an essential step in maturity and in refining our search for happiness. The one common denominator, amongst all humankind, is the desire for happiness. For those whose lives take a spiritual bent, a basic premise is arrived at: this world will never be a source for lasting happiness—not ever.

The true aspirant knows that what produces real, lasting, happiness is communion with God; the Self, united with the infinite Being, is eternal and is filled with supreme Consciousness and Bliss.

Due to the physical body's tendency to get sick, grow old, and die, this world can never fulfill this promise. Prosperity and situations in life are ever in flux; every high is followed by a low. So it is with all things created; the law of duality always applies, without exception. The discriminating devotee knows that whatever is born will die, that anything external to the Self will one day fall away, and that there is no pleasure or satisfaction in this worldly realm that will not lose its savor over time.

Each individual has the right to any theory he or she chooses for attaining lasting happiness. But, one thing is certain, if the essence of that theory and its practice does not have at its very core the eternal Being, Consciousness, and Bliss of God, it will fail to supply lasting happiness.

January 31

BOTH FULLY HUMAN AND FULLY DIVINE

Mother Hamilton, 1981.

On our way down to Mother's gravesite for the 24th anniversary of her Mahasamadhi, we were discussing a new book we were reading on organizing and tidying. On the surface, this may not seem to be a "spiritual" subject to be thinking about at that time, but it did remind me of Mother and her practical approach to life.

Once, Mother asked me to come over to help her organize her storage closet at her condominium. She was always very careful with her things and she told stories of how different items came to her, their history, their value, etc. This may seem like materialism to some, but Mother was teaching us to have balance in all ways.

Mother knew how to organize. She was a wonderful and inventive interior decorator. Once she said that if she came back again, she would like to do interior design professionally. Then, she added, that of course in her present role as a Guru, she was helping to decorate the interiors of disciples' minds and hearts. This emphasis on physical beauty and organization disturbed some people's concept of what a spiritual teacher should be focused on, but Mother was not the least bit apologetic. As a fully realized spiritual Master, Mother was at ease with this world. She recognized that being accomplished in this world, creating beauty, and charging adequate pay for work done, were all important in making a person whole and balanced.

There are some who teach spiritual living and espouse non-materialism while themselves living quite materialistic lives. The fact is, we live in a material world, and to find the right balance and realize it is all God should be our goal; not paint ourselves into a hypocritical corner. As Papa wrote, even a sadhu wandering penniless may be possessive of his water pot, prideful over wearing an orange cloth, or take offense because someone does not pay him due homage as a "holy person." Attachment is a subtle and treacherous companion.

There is the instructive instance in the life of Janaka, a realized king. When a boy was sent to Janaka to be instructed, he was dismissive of the king who was surrounded by courtiers and politicians. The boy, who had only a few holy books with him, was invited by the king to sit with him. Suddenly a fire broke out in the palace and messengers frantically inquired of the king what to do. He told them he was talking to this boy about spiritual subjects and he should not be disturbed. Finally, the unabated fire crept toward the two who were engrossed in talking about God. As the flames moved toward the boy's holy books, he carefully moved them away. After maneuvering his books away from the flames a couple of times, the king commented, "What! My entire palace burns but my mind and talk are engrossed in God. Meanwhile, you are concerned with your books. Tell me, who is attached?" The boy recognized the greatness of Janaka and was humbled.

The Master Jesus told us, "Be in the world, but not of the world" (John 17:16–18 adapted). Truly we must have a place to live, food to eat, clothes to wear, handle money, and, depending on the work we have to do, we may have a few or many possessions. Can we live like Mother Hamilton in this world: create beauty and order, but without attachment?

As we encircled Mother's gravesite to pay her homage, we listened to Janice Stevenson's piano renditions of two of Mother's chants, *Hymn to Krishna* and *God's Lullaby*. The first is an esoteric song to an ancient and holy avatar, the other written as a lullaby for Gari, her baby son; both beautiful and both heartfelt. The songs echoed in our hearts as a melodious and fitting tribute to our universal Mother who always told us that she was both fully human and fully Divine.

February 7

PART ONE: THE JOY OF TIDYING

Lakshmi, Goddess of Prosperity,
painting by Raja Ravi Varma, 1910.**

An aspirant was telling me about struggles to organize and get things in order. This is something I have also had a great desire to master in this lifetime. It seems to be an ever-elusive goal. I know that it is both a skill set and it has many mental and emotional layers to it as well. During our time of talking, we made an agreement with each other to set a goal for March 31st to have our houses in order, as well as living wills and last wills.

When you set a clear goal, and ask God for His assistance, then it is amazing how help comes in so many unexpected and delightful ways. Carla came across a book, *The Life-Changing Magic of Tidying Up,* by Marie Kondo. We decided to make a study of this book, and if it made sense, then to put it to work. As Marie points out, we are trained in so many things in life, but how to tidy up and organize our home is not one of them; we are just supposed to know how.

Our abundance in life produces great challenges for us. For many of us starvation is not the problem, it is to discover the right foods and the right amounts of food. It is not the lack of information, but it is choosing what information we take in so that we are not swimming in too much of it. And the amount of books, papers, clothes, and general stuff we have can create a state of clutter that can become chaotic, frustrating, and inefficient; it also blunts appreciation and joy in having those things. Learning to manage abundance is one of the great modern privileges we have.

Marie Kondo has made a lifetime study of organizing and being tidy. An unusual child, she would rush home from school to devour a new magazine on home decor, always with an eye toward efficiency articles. While somewhat obsessive in the preoccupation, she devised schemes and tried out many methods. What balanced her in her drive was her focus on what things gave her joy to have in her home.

It is this theme of finding joy and happiness in things you have when organizing and tidying your home that makes all the difference in her approach. By taking a complete category, such as all your tops (shirts, sweatshirts, sweaters, etc.) and laying them all out, then handling each one and asking yourself, "Does this give me joy?" You keep only those things that give you joy and discard the rest. What you end up with in the end is being surrounded by only those things that bring you joy.

She even has methods for how to fold your clothes, she is Japanese after all (the land of origami), and you think, "Oh I don't know about that." Then you try it, and lo and behold, it works! The first category was strangely hard to do. But since then, this feeling of joy in choosing and organizing has become contagious, and I find now that I want more of it. And, in the end, who does not want more joy?

February 12

PART TWO: THE JOY OF TIDYING 2

Albert Einstein, 1941.**
"Everything should be made as
simple as possible, but not simpler."
—ALBERT EINSTEIN

The response to the posting on *The Joy of Tidying* has been tre-mendous; it hit a real need. Already the amount of clothes gone from a number of households has filled up dozens of garbage bags. This means greater organization and enjoyment for the givers, and it has released thousands of items to new recipi-ents who will find joy in them.

The things you have are manifestations of your consciousness, so this is not just stuff, useful tools, or clutter; these are all items that are connected to you. As a result, when you make changes in your home, you change your consciousness. When you release things that are no longer right for you, you feel light, free and have renewed energy.

We all need things in life, clothing for warmth and style, shelter, books, papers, tools for accomplishing our tasks in life, and entertainment. What is the right amount for one is different than for another, but we all recognize clutter when we have it, which is having things that are not right for us or having too much of it.

Find the right balance that allows the winds of heaven to move through all parts of your life, uninhibited; recognize that clutter blocks that movement. Here are a couple of points made by the author, Marie Kondo (*The Life-Changing Magic of Tidying Up*), said in my own words:

- Books are for reading, if you are not going to re-read a book or read it for the first time (you have had it for six months and not read it yet) then pass it on, even if it is new. Let someone else enjoy the book you will probably never open.

- The joy of receiving a gift may be in the exchange, itself. If, after this exchange, the item does not give you joy, then pass it on. Know the gift has already fulfilled its purpose when you received it through the thoughtfulness and effort the giver made in presenting it to you. Real friends would not want you hanging on to something they gave you if it does not give you real joy.

- A few pictures will remind you of a past event. Having boxes of badly taken pictures that you will "someday" go through will not bring you joy, nor will you ever go through them. Sort them now and keep only the cream of the crop.

- Keep papers only as long as it takes to deal with them. When you respond to a letter or pay a bill, let the paper go; don't keep them a minute longer. And don't keep extra buttons from new clothes (when have you ever used that button?), even instruction manuals you can look up online—let them all go.

- Make a place for <u>everything</u> you have. Give it a home and then find joy in returning it to its home when you are done with it.

Many of us think of organizing and tidying up as a hassle, overwhelming or never really possible. Connecting this process to feeling joy, freedom, and clarity of consciousness brings new elements to what may seem a vexing and perpetual problem.

February 18

MORE JOY

Carla Hickenbottom sorting clothes.

More and more individuals have worked on discarding those items that no longer bring them joy. There are some things that come up when doing so that I would like to comment on. One is the material from past classes I have given; what to do with handouts from those classes?

There are a few, like Carla, who will actually go back and review past class notes, study them, and work to integrate them into their daily life. However, I know the reality is that those are few in number, no matter how well intentioned we may be.

The real value for many is the experience of the retreat or class itself; the insights, feelings, and upliftment that come at the time and immediately after. For many, the purpose is already fulfilled in just coming to such an event. While the handouts were very valuable at the time, that moment has come and gone and re-reading the material will not have the same effect as it did originally. If that describes you, then you may let the handouts go.

This issue has come up for several aspirants, and it tugs at the heart and soul to think of discarding these papers. The question that comes to mind is, "Am I being disloyal or disrespectful in thinking of getting rid of them?" Go inside, if you honestly feel the only reason for keeping them is guilt, then let them go. If you feel real joy in having them, then by all means keep them. You may always request a digital copy from Carla for any materials from any past class or retreat.

When you let go of anything, it adds great meaning when you give gratitude for the service those materials rendered you and the experiences you had in the class. In India, when a sacred image has been damaged and can no longer be the focus for worshipping Divine Consciousness, then the image is taken to the Ganges, or some sacred river, and submerged into the flowing stream. You might like to have a ceremony and to give a moment of gratitude for how these materials served you at the time of the retreat, then give them a heartfelt send-off.

Another issue that comes up for different ones is when very few items in possession give any joy. There is a recognition that he or she has brought things into the home for utilitarian reasons, but joy was not part of it. Now you may have filed some insurance papers or other items that should be kept, but you cannot say they give you joy, except in knowing you should have them. However, there may be many things, such as clothes and furniture, that are in your home by choice, but you have no real love for them. Then the question comes, "Will I have anything, or enough left if I get rid of all of this?"

It may require you to become creative when you let certain things go. You can make it fun and interesting to see how to get along without something by being innovative, which may make you feel more alive and less encumbered. To see unloved things leave lifts a burden from you and opens the way for more things to come; things that you will really love. It could be you just have too much darn stuff, and so much can go out the door that you will not ever miss; even if there is some fear beforehand that you can't do without it.

There is no doubt about it, this is a purging. And there are those reporting that when they purge their house, they lose weight, have added clarity of mind, make decisions in other areas of life more easily, and even have signs of physical purging similar to a fast. This is really fascinating and powerful stuff!

It is a great way to get the energy moving in your own life. If you feel stuck right now, thoroughly purge your home of anything that does not produce joy.

I continue to be impressed with Marie Kondo's book, *The Life-Changing Magic of Tidying Up*, and I encourage you to read it even if you feel you are good at getting rid of things because of her know-how, the feeling and spirit that comes with her words, her well-considered and deep knowledge of the subject, and her emphasis on more joy.

February 20

PART ONE: CHOOSING
ONLY JOYFUL THOUGHTS

Papa Ramdas in Joy-filled Bliss.

I f we apply the lessons of tidying to our thinking, then we could start on the first of two stages of internal house clearing—discarding any thoughts that do not bring us joy. Recognizing that if thought is the creative powerhouse that directs our emotions, energy, and activity, then choosing only joyful thoughts and the supreme bliss of God is the only course that makes sense.

Yet we see that this is not what many people do. Instead, they remain focused on those thoughts that produce unhappiness; with so many of those things outside the direct control of the individual. So, instead of choosing joy, there is too much choosing of suffering instead.

This can seem crazy for anyone to choose unhappiness, and yet we know from first-hand experience that we do exactly that. The natural question comes, "Why?" The answers can vary, but it comes down to the same thing—a part of us thinks a negative thought will make us safe and happy. For instance, a state of depression can seem like a safe place to retreat. A child may seek out a closet, make a nest of blankets and pillows inside and close the closet door to darken the room. Inside the closet all the chaos, shame, and fear disappear. Depression can initially feel like that closet, all safe and warm.

And every other "negative" behavior has a root cause in seeking happiness—but in all the wrong places. Again, "Why?" Because you are not one whole person yet. You have many parts to your self, parts that vie with one another for fulfillment of varied needs. The key to resolving this inner conflict can be found in learning some basic spiritual principles, and then teaching them to all the various parts of yourself.

One such principle is to choose joy. Absolute joy is ultimately a spiritual gift, not just "luck of the draw" or just for a fortunate few, but grace that comes to all. However, the key to having joy is to be really open to receiving it. There are many who say they want happiness, but parts of them do not believe they deserve it, or if they get it, then it will be taken from them: "So (goes the reasoning), better not to even think that happiness can be mine."

However, there is no stopping a determined soul, especially true when individual will is united with Divine Will! Decide to choose joy, discard every other thought, and open the door to grace and real joy; Bliss flows to you, of this, I am sure.

Flame Exercise: When a thought comes to you and it does not spark joy, then discard it. See with your mind's eye a flame

12 to 14 inches in front of you, then send the unwanted thought into this flame—the Light of God. See those thoughts you are discarding flowing into the flame. See the flame consume the thought and take it up and away—purified in those flames.

In this way you can choose only thoughts that give you joy. Let everything else go. Moods, unhealthy desires, compulsions, and negativity can be gotten rid of, beginning now! Decide to think only of Light, universal Love, and ever-new Joy, and change your life, never to be the same.

February 24

PART TWO: FINDING A PLACE FOR JOY

Krishna and Radha filled with joyful
activity, Akshardham Temple, India.

Finding a place for every chosen thought is the second stage after choosing only joyful thoughts. As in Marie Kondo's book, tidying is broken into two parts to be done in sequence, so may we look at tidying our minds with the same kind of intention that we would use in our homes.

Once having discarded all thoughts that do not give a spark of joy we then focus on finding a place for every thought that remains. These thoughts are intentions that are made to serve us.

Many people simply let their thoughts roam at will creating chaos and pain. They often blame the world for not fulfilling their every wish without ever taking stock of their own creative power.

Think of your home when you are only surrounded by things that give you joy and there is space for every single thing you have. How pleasing and calming it is to have a closet, drawer, counter-top, tool chest or garden shed that looks spacious and has a particular place for everything you have.

Now, take a look at the various tasks and occupations which make up your life. Even as Sri Yukteswarji worked with Master to better discipline him to be regular in his habits, so you will observe that you benefit from having regular structure to your days and your nights.

Each person is unique in how much structure suits his or her personality and needs. Be keenly observant about how your thoughts either serve you or are a disservice. Lay out all the activities you have during the day. Ask yourself, does this activity bring me joy? Discarding those things that do not.

There are tasks in life that we may say, "Well, I do not love doing the dishes; however, if I don't wash and put the dishes away it robs me of joy; therefore, I have to say that it does give me joy in the end."

There are habits that can rob you of the joy you would normally have for an activity. For instance, if you are often late getting to places, then on your way there you easily get frustrated at small delays, feel anxious when arriving, and frustrate those who were on time. There is a cost to this habit, and you pay it. Having not allowed the "space" of time its proper place, you have robbed yourself of joy.

Perhaps you somehow always feel rushed to meditate or are too tired at night to do so; spend money you do not have or that you cannot easily afford; through fear, you do not say what is true for you; and rush through projects and make many mistakes which you have to redo or have fear others will discover. These are all areas where your thinking habits do not serve you, and even though you would say that each activity brings you joy, the fact you have not given what you are doing its proper space in time, means it takes the joy out of it.

One thing that may become vividly clear when you lay your day out in front of you is that you commit yourself to too many things. Even when taken individually each activity brings you joy, taken as a whole it does not. You must be willing to discard those thought/expectations that crowd your life. Learn to give adequate space to those things you have given priority.

At a time when we have so many "time savers," equipment and technology that make life so much easier, we too often live with stress and feeling pressured for time. This is because we have not discarded those thoughts and activities that, in the end, do not bring joy because we have not found a proper place for everything we wish to do.

There may be many areas in which you load yourself up with expectations because you want to do it all, or you have a desire to please others, or you may have a fear of being left out, or that you will miss out. Or, perhaps you load your time with mindless entertainment to "unwind." These are the areas that benefit from carefully considering what to discard.

Just like you have the challenge of learning to deal with having so many belongings in your life, you also have the privilege of choosing from so many possibilities of what to do. Most of us have come a long way from working on a farm from sunup to sundown, with little time or energy for anything else. How we choose to spend time must be done consciously; to choose joy, and to carefully find time for all the things that really matter brings balance.

Prioritizing and discarding lesser activities makes room for taking more time to commune with God, to complete projects, paint, write, take walks, or be early for appointed times. Finding a place for everything that brings you joy means that you can comfortably fit those things into your days and nights; this reduces stress and increases your joy.

God once gave me a mantra for a life that felt too busy to do everything: "I have plenty of time to do all the important things in my life." This requires that I find what brings me real heart and soul joy, what is most important, and make that the priority. Time can actually expand to find a proper place for all those important things when you discard the rest.

Here is to a more joyful life where everything important in your life has a place and a spacious fit.

February 26

FULFILLING YOUR HEART'S DESIRE

Rose Blossoms: Divine Mother's love of color and variety.

Like many anniversaries in life, a birthday gives time for reflection. Like an eagle flying high above sees a person down below and can look far back, know where the person is now, and can gaze forward to see what is to come, I have had the privilege of God showing me many of my past incarnations. Like a light switch thrown and a room lit up, a revelation can be given in which the gist of a whole lifetime can be given in an instant, or perhaps just a significant moment is seen. When it is God who is showing you, whatever is shown will relate to something you are going through in that moment, and it is given to you to help release you from the past.

I can look back to many experiences that have all gone into making me who I am today. And not all of them are good, or perfect, but then some of them show signs of compassion and clarity. In what I have been given, there has been more suffering than overcoming. That is because it is those things I have done wrong, or have traumatized me, that have held me back. In order to be released from these things that follow me from lifetime to lifetime, I must absorb the lesson intended, not always the one I learned at that time.

Perhaps the greatest revelation that has come from these experiences is that the law of cause and effect, the boomerang of Karma, is not meant as punishment, but rather it occurs to teach compassion. If I do something despicable to another without real consideration for how that action affects them, then those same actions will be visited upon me. When they come to me, I understand what suffering is produced by that action. When this happens enough, I will see myself in the happiness or suffering of all others, for no one is a stranger to me. There is nothing another does that I have not done, in some version, and there is no pain another may have that has not been mine at some time. My vision becomes universalized. This is the lesson of compassion my past has taught me.

In the present, I am reading the newly published Cross and Lotus Journal, after having gone over it many times when proofing it. In reading Mother's Easter Talk I find myself carried into her living presence; her words, thoughts, and spiritual experiences are not just reacting in my brain, but through my whole Being. She is telling my story. At the time she gave the talk she was showing me the way. Now, as I read her words, she is telling the way that I have come. When Mother ordained me a Yogacharya she said that I had been through nearly all the experiences she had been through—I was quite surprised when she said that.

What was very important in her statement was—"nearly." And, in fact, there were many experiences yet to go through, some of them unimaginable to me at the time. I think for the most part it is best for us to not know everything we will have to go through before-hand! However, through those experiences, I am now able to enjoy a communion with God that does, as Sri Yukteswarji said it would, fulfill my heart's desire. I melt in gratitude to God and Guru for making this possible. I know in every cell of my being that God-experience is the source of every happiness, and it is separation from Him that makes suffering. My soul melts and merges with Him, then He re-animates me to serve Him in all forms, and it is all His play. This—I know.

Looking forward I only know that there is much work to do. I know with every fiber of my being that Mother's words, the truth that came at such a high price, must go out in order to help this world to change. She speaks to all the Christian world, telling them of the original teachings and the meaning of Jesus. She also bridges the teachings of Jesus to reach out to every man, woman, and child the world over, those belonging to every religion—for she tells a story with universal significance. This world stands on the verge of becoming more universal, we see signs of it every-where; yet the oppositional force does not go quietly. Dedicated souls must first tread the way themselves, and then be willing to share the Light now shining through their forms.

I see a world that tempers individuality, competition, and striving with compassion, internally derived joy, and universal vision. God proves through Nature that He loves individual expression, as Divine Mother manifests through so many different kinds of flowers, so much beauty, so many colors, and outrageous patterns. So, She must love Her individuality in humanity. When we realize that every individual is part of one complete puzzle, and for the picture to be complete no piece of the puzzle can be discarded or treated with disrespect, then we will have taken a giant step forward to universalizing our vision.

So, as the eagle swoops earthward, and on this day that I ostensibly celebrate my birth, the birth of a body that is simply one of many this soul has inhabited, I wish that all your heart's desires be fulfilled. And, I do happen to know a secret—realizing God will satisfy your heart, completely.

March 4

MAKING ROOM FOR GOD: ONLY KEEPING THE THINGS I LOVE

Yogacharya David and Angela.

I want to share something Angela Victory just sent me (used with her permission). Angela is one of many who have embraced this process of tidying wholeheartedly. She has experienced a deepening spiritual connection through choosing only things that bring her a spark of joy. Strangely, this focus on material things makes us feel closer to God; we feel a new and lighter energy throughout our home. My hope is that you will enjoy Angela's writing, but more than that, you will be inspired.[4]

---

4   Book Reference: *The Life-Changing Magic of Tidying Up,* Marie Kondo.

This method of tidying has, and continues to be, an inspiration that has preoccupied my mind. Driving home the other day I felt driven, so so driven to conquer the stuff in my home and my life. It's hard to really convey this feeling other than to say it was a burning desire. Not something that takes energy away from my constitution, but brings me everything I need. Drawing on the life-force energy from behind: it's calm, it's strong, and it's wonderful. My whole body resonates with letting these attachments go—without pain, but with joy!

I never imagined that I would ever have gotten here in my life . . . gone is my attachment to my worn white leather baby shoes; still in their perfect condition cardboard box. They were bought on a special trip that my mom and dad took to Hastings Street; quality baby shoes for my feet. These shoes were kept by my mother, and now kept by me—moved from box to box, location to location, from her home to my home.

Recently, with this cleaning-up-my-life obsession, I looked at those baby shoes in a new light, and I said, "I know exactly where you need to be, you need to be in my loving pile of donations." The transition seemed so simple, and then it led to Barbie dolls (one being my authentic Princess Leia doll), and clothes my mother wore on her honeymoon, my beautiful yellow-golden grade 12 signature high school vintage jacket—I was an art class chic artist.

This jacket: it was so individual and I loved it. I could still wear it today, but I feel more strongly about donating it than trying to find a place in my closet to keep it—and for how long? Forever? I am not the jacket, yet it has defined me. I saw in my mind a girl searching for vintage things in today's world, and her coming across that jacket and seeing the potential in it—and her having the opportunity to find it—and it now defining her. I joyfully donated it.

The jacket brings fond feelings, like the feeling I get when I reflect on God. I close my eyes slightly and I remember the feeling to be "connected." Wearing my jacket, or keeping the jacket in the back of my closet is not my connection with Him—that feeling of connection comes from tuning in directly with Him: there is where the love is, that is my gratitude.

Keeping only the things I love—it can be described as a switch, a switch being turned on. Moments before I was so attached to so many things, and then I was not. It doesn't mean that I don't love so many things that I donated, but they no longer serve a purpose in my life.

My stuff was actually starting to make me sick: giving me headaches all the time, I was feeling like I couldn't see properly, a foggy cloud around me, I was bothered and feeling worn out. Today, as these things that no longer give me a spark of joy leave my house I feel fresh air around me, I feel my mind opening up and making room for a larger altar for God.

It reminds me of the story of the man who had royalty (God) come to his house, but the man felt his house wasn't ready to receive such a royal guest. So, I can use my body to physically move things out of this house to make room—there isn't a greater love I know of than to make room for God.

I know that my mom wanted help tidying up her stuff, and we never really knew how, or what to do with it. But now, with the concept of only keeping things that bring us joy—I get it!

I opened my dishwasher this morning to unload my clean dishes. I looked on the top shelf and I looked on the bottom shelf inside the washer, and all I saw were all my favorite dishes—joy! It was a thrill to put them away, not a task. I love each and every one of them: the Anthropologie mugs, my mom's glass jug for sauce, simple Ikea tumblers, French style plates, white plates, a water jug for two, shiny matching silverware and my vintage made-in-England dish—that is the dish that I set my Rice Krispy squares in. The evidence was right in front of me, and I smiled big!

To be connected with my things means to be connected with God. If I am connected with absolutely everything I own, then I hope to be connected with God in absolutely every way as well.

March 20

Truth Will Make You Free

Swami Sri Yukteswarji.**

I came into this life and gave others a great deal of power over me. What someone else thought or said would have great power, more power than what I thought. This can be termed being shy, having low self-esteem, or a lack of confidence, etc. It is a terrible way to live.

There was a time when I was in a mediation partnership, we taught a roomful of lawyers and social worker-types the skills of mediation. At the end of the five-day course, we asked for written feedback. Ninety-nine percent of the feedback was incredibly positive, such as "One of best things I have ever done, life chang-ing," etc. Once in a while someone would say, "Not really what I was looking for." Somehow this one feedback carried all the weight, wiping out all the good comments. I knew my reaction was way out of proportion, but there it was.

In my training in behavioral sciences there was a phrase that stuck with me, "**feedback is information, not definition**." Being open to feedback was an important part of my Master's degree program. At first, I went easy on others in the class, hop-ing they would do the same for me. When the feedback I got was honest, sometimes blunt, I thought, "Ok, kid gloves are off, this is what I really think." I strove to make the feedback clean and clear, not filled with anger or hurt or prejudice, but accurate and useful and I did not hold back.

What a refreshing breath of fresh air! How rarely we get clean and clear feedback in this world. Either others do not say what they really think, feel, and want, or it is so filled with some per-sonal attack that it is really more about the other person than us. Why is it so hard for us to be simply truthful, and why is it so hard for us to receive what someone else thinks, feels, or wants?

It really comes down to having confidence in what "I think, feel, and want." When I have faith and confidence in my own judg-ments, then what others think will not be *swallowed whole,* rather I will listen openly to what another thinks, and measure it by what I know to be true. I use my reason and my intuition to sense the truth. What is it I have faith and confidence in? Not that I am per-fect, rather I have faith and confidence in the fact that I am a good person, well intentioned, and that if somehow I make a mistake, my sincerity will get me back on track with truth.

Truth, then, becomes the transcendent factor that rises above personalities. To stand in the way of truth by being overly self-conscious means that ego triumphs. Truth may come from any source: a child, an elderly person, a stranger, madman, or a belligerent. To recognize truth requires you to have a calm, clear mind focused on knowing the truth when you see, hear or feel it.

Your spiritual practice of being centered in the Self and attuned to truth will greatly enable you to put truth over personality; you transcend ego. Put truth first, and the truth will make you free.

March 25

TRAVIS RANEY, GRADUATION SPEECH

Yogacharya David and Travis Raney on Graduation Night.

We recently attended the graduation ceremony for Travis and I was greatly pleased when he gave the speech for the graduating class, as well as being awarded top honors in the class as voted on by the students. Carla said it was the best graduation speech she has ever heard; I thought you would enjoy reading an excerpted copy. Travis said that when he attended the graduation of the previous year's class a year before, this speech flowed into his mind in almost its entirety right then.

Travis:

Good evening, thank you all for coming to support us tonight.

There have been so many people who've helped us all make it here to graduation tonight and I would like to express our gratitude to as many of them as possible.

First and foremost, I would like to personally give thanks for Divine Providence, without which—I would not be here tonight.

To all of our friends and families who have been so supportive in so many ways . . . .

Well, we are finally here at graduation, it has been such a long path, it has been a path filled with sacrifice, with countless hours studying, with pressure, with stress, and sometimes even tears.

And I just wanted to make sure that I stated for the record that I never cried . . . I find what works best for me is a special technique I developed where I just bottle up all my stress and emotions deep inside, and hope something good happens.

I see some worried faces out there, and I can see my family all nodding their heads in agreement. Don't worry people, it's just supposed to be a joke, I promise BTC doesn't teach the bottle technique, and I do have some healthy outlets to deal with stress. In fact—self-care is an important concept emphasized throughout this nursing program.

If we fail to advocate for ourselves and for our own well-being, it is possible that we can become overburdened with stress. Finding time to recharge ourselves with healthy stress relieving activities is essential to maintaining balance and longevity in the nursing field. For if we neglect to care for ourselves in this way, we will likely be unable to provide the highest standard of nursing care that our patients deserve.

We have worked so hard to get to where we are today, and we should all be proud of our hard work. That being said, I encourage you not to fall into a mindset of entitlement, but rather let us look at our achievements in this way . . . That we have proven ourselves to be safe, competent, and compassionate nurses, worthy of the privilege of serving the infirmed at an RN level. For care-giving truly is an honor and a privilege.

We have reached a higher level of education, and I know that all of you are going to be great nurses. But what is greatness, and what does it mean to be great?

I would like to share with you a short story about a group of students similar to our own small class. This group was talking amongst themselves when a dispute arose among them as to which was considered to be greatest. Upon overhearing this conversation among his students, their teacher replied in so many words:

"The greatest among you will be your servant."

It is my hope that we take this spirit of servitude and selflessness into the nursing profession. When we are with our patients let us set aside our differences; let us set aside anything that might be going on in our personal lives and just serve them.

Bringing medicine and monitoring vital signs are important aspects of nursing, but bringing a compassionate smile, a joyful, humorous attitude, and Love to your patients is what will facilitate healing of the whole person: body, mind, and spirit. Making a difference in such a large world can sometimes seem like an overwhelming task, but let us not become weary in doing what is good, what is just, and what is in the best interest of our patients.

But what can one person really do to effect significant change?

I feel that Mother Teresa caught a glimpse of the Truth and spoke of it when she stated: **"It is not how much we do, but how much love we put in the doing. It is not how much we give, but how much love is put in the giving."**

I would like to finish with a few words spoken by an English social reformer, statistician, and the founder of modern nursing, Florence Nightingale. This woman served as a nurse manager during the Crimean war in 1854 where she would make rounds to the wounded soldiers at night using an olive oil lamp. The Florence Nightingale olive oil lamp has since become an international symbol of nursing. In 1860 Nightingale opened the first scientifically-based nursing school at St Thomas' Hospital in London. This laid the foundation that the future of professional nursing would build upon. Here are a few of her words, and I quote:

"I would rather, ten times, die in the surf, heralding the way to a new world, than stand idly on the shore."

So, get out there boldly; let your light shine before others; bring compassion, bring patience, bring humility, and above all else—love one another unconditionally.

Thank you.

March 27

COME, FOLLOW ME

Christ at 33, painting by
Heinrich Hofmann, 1889.**

I recently gave a talk entitled, Jesus Was a Jew. It reminded me of a story Mother once told of a little girl who came home from Sunday School and exclaimed to her mother, "Mommy, they said Jesus was a Jew!" The mother reassured her child saying, "Never mind dear, we all know he was a good Methodist!"

We all look at the Master through the lens of our own minds, conditioned by time and circumstance. We see artists' renditions of Jesus with blond hair and blue eyes, fair skinned, all which would have been highly unusual for a Jew of his time. It makes many comfortable to think of him as "someone like us;" as a "good Methodist."

Even the teachings of the various churches that follow him would have been foreign to Jesus, certainly many of his followers would have been astounded. The notion of the trinity became officially recognized 300 years after the time of Jesus, and for many of his direct followers to think of him as one of three aspects of one God would have been news to many of them at the time. Even three hundred years later, it took some pretty fancy reasoning to work it out, with many tries before there came an acceptable version. Yet today, it is held as sacrosanct for all true believers.

There is no evidence Jesus intended to start a new religion. He called upon those he healed to keep secret what had happened, he pointed his teachings toward loving God and one's fellow man, and his focus was upon strengthening faith in God, whom he called Abba, Father. He taught in Jewish synagogues and in the great Temple, and strove to challenge those who ran the temple to be pure and upright. He did not break with Jewish tradition, in fact he said he was the fulfillment of its promise.

When Paul, not a direct disciple, asked for permission many years after the time of Jesus to initiate others who were not Jews into these teachings, it created quite a stir. James, and even Peter rejected the idea. Later Peter had a dream in which he received sanction for Paul to do so. The point is, the direct disciples did not see themselves as anything other than Jews at the time. Paul even came up with his own fancy reasoning so that new male converts did not have to be physically circumcised, a Jewish rite, but that their faith in Jesus made them circumcised. Why go through the trouble of reasoning this out unless it was thought that becoming a Christian was essentially becoming Jewish.

And why do I now point out these self-evident facts? It is to focus on what is essential to the life and teachings of this Jewish rabbi. Even his breaking of bread and sharing of wine was a rite already established by the Essenes. While Jesus borrowed heavily from the ancient tradition in which he was born, he also articulated the greatest spiritual principles to be found anywhere. This man, whose background we are told so little, gave us the keys to finding the kingdom of heaven, only to be found within.

What he gave us was so much more than a new religion, he gave us the Truth! He taught us to live the life of a true spiritual being, to love God first, surrender to His will, and to serve our fellow man, even unto death. Jesus taught us how to truly live. I say he taught "us," because he teaches us still through the stories of his life, and the power of his words that resonate around the world.

"Come, follow me," (Matthew 4:19) Jesus said to his direct disciples, and he says this to all of us. To follow him means to live as he lived, to know what he knew, to be even as he was; a Son of God. "Follow me," not in blind belief, but see with your own eyes, hear with your own ears, know with your own mind, the same as he saw, heard, and knew—his heavenly Father. He calls to us even now, "Come, follow me."

March 30

SATSANG

Swami Ramdas (center), Mother Hamilton and Ralph
Hamilton (left) with Anandashram devotees, India.**

Satsang is coming together for the purpose of spiritual upliftment and transformation. Ultimately satsang is to become
established in the true Self, or God-consciousness.

These last few days we have been in Ashland to be with the
Group here. When kindred spirits come together, the feeling of
love and joy is palpable in the air. It is a time of quickening as
those here feel a purifying power that changes lives and helps all
progress in spiritualizing the mind.

When I started this path, I was very much alone on it, friends
at the time were not interested in this unusual quest I found
myself on. And in meeting Mother, necessity of work in distant
places, and of going to college elsewhere, kept me from knowing

many of those who gathered around Mother. Add to that, I was so lifted up when around Mother that communicating with others was well-nigh impossible.

Gradually that has all changed, but the meaning and the purpose of satsang has not. Only now I am able to operate in the body and be in a state of satsang; merged with the Self, even while with others. How wonderful to surcharge the atmosphere with chanting God's holy Nam, feeling the power of Truth flow through this form throughout a talk, and then to feel His current of love, laughter, and joy as we gather around potluck food and sit in the sunshine.

Perhaps it was best in the beginning that it was a lonely path, for that made me find an inner connection with God and Guru that was independent of those I was around. But today, my heart bursts with joy in being with sincere aspirants in a spirit of upliftment and transformation. Whether we find ourselves alone or with other devotees, may we always find that connection with God, but what a real treasure it is when sincere souls gather together in satsang.

April 3

THE REDEMPTION OF CAIN AND ABEL

Abel and Cain.**

A new revelation came this early morning. As we know, Adam represents reason and Eve represents feeling and they are seduced by the downward facing serpent of attraction to the senses. As a result, they remove themselves from the Garden of Eden in which they easily commune with God and live harmoniously with Divine and Nature's laws.

Adam and Eve have two offspring, Cain and Abel. The two represent the dual nature, positive and negative attributes of the son of man. Abel is the desire to be in harmony with God and the fruit of his actions pleases Him. Cain represents ignorance and goes against Divine Harmony. Cain becomes jealous of Abel's easy relationship with God and he "kills" Abel. The negative tendencies of Cain rise up leading to jealousy, anger, and murder, and the good tendencies of Abel die, are no longer evident in consciousness.

The mark of Cain is those tendencies of self-absorption, jealousy, anger, and greed. He may be known by those tendencies and is marked by them wherever he exists. Cain kills the good tendencies; however, the good tendencies cry out from the earth, they remain in the consciousness as an echo, and cannot be completely eliminated. As a result of going against Divine Will and killing good tendencies, Cain goes further away from Divine Harmony and lives among those who have the son-of-man only.

This is a tragic and wonderful description of what happens to all souls who have descended into darkness. The good news, the Gospel, is that there is redemption for all who "receive" Christ Consciousness by following in the Way of the Cross, or live in self-surrender.

Go forward in time to when Jesus was nailed to the cross, with two thieves on either side of him. One thief wants to go with Jesus to heaven that day; the other is mocking the Christ and wants a miracle only to save his life. These two thieves are Abel and Cain, and their tendencies have remained the same. The one desires to do the will of God; the other is filled with anger and recrimination.

After their deaths, both thieves have their legs broken, but Jesus legs are not broken. That is, the power of the good and evil tendencies within man is overcome, this allows the son-of-man to ascend and fully manifest as the Son-of-God. Jesus told the good thief that he would be with him in heaven that day; that is, the dual nature must be broken, but in the end the good tendencies abide in the Son-of-God, only now the Son-of-God is not identified with the ego nature of doing good.

Through the Mystical Crucifixion the serpent fully rises to the top of the tree, or the cross, which represents the man or woman whose will is fully surrendered to God's will. This ascension reverses what was done by Adam and Eve in going with the downward facing serpent on the tree of life, and it ultimately restores man to God.

This morning, on the day of a full moon and Good Friday, God has shown me this connection between Cain and Abel and the two thieves on the cross. How good God is, how sublime and perfect are the teachings in these stories. These stories are ostensibly about history dating back thousands of years, but even more meaningfully, these stories are descriptions of the son-of-man nature and the Son-of-God nature residing in every man and woman the world over. It is the story of the redemption of every individual who would seek out Christ Consciousness, by what-ever name it may be called. It is the story of you and me.

April 6

YOUR BIRTH HERITAGE

Christ Emerging from the tomb.

Monday after a full Easter weekend, Saturday Meditation, watching *Jesus of Nazareth*[5] with devotees, Sunday Service, potluck, and an Easter egg hunt with the little ones, I have a happy "hangover;" a feeling of Bliss and well-being that is pervasive within and without. This feeling once again

---

5   A 1972 film. ITC Entertainment, RAI. Directed by Franco Zeffirelli.

emphasizes the principle of being mindful of the after-effect from any activity.

Observing the after-effect of any action puts us in a position of learning from our experience. The first taste of alcohol or a drag of a cigarette produces a physical reaction of distaste; the body trying to rid itself of toxic substances. We override these sensations due to peer pressure or with a desire of getting some experience from it.

In this way we repeat doing things the body initially rejects, but then starts to crave. In addition, the next morning, say after drinking, we have a hangover that is most unpleasant. With repeated experiences, all fine sensitivities natural to the individual are dulled; being out of harmony with God's and Nature's laws is accepted as the norm.

Now what is wrong is made to be right, what is healthy is seen as something to be avoided. This produces physical, mental, and spiritual dis-ease. How far we descend from knowing what is right; how hard we work to justify doing wrong.

This creation was made to be enjoyed in the Bliss of God, not to get entangled in sticky webs of desire and attachment. With a polluted mind, finding original innocence is not easy or clear, not because this knowledge was not with us from the beginning, but because we have become so habituated to wrong living.

Learning to be a keen observer of the after-effect of actions is the beginning of wisdom. You do not need to look far in order to see which habits do not produce joy: too much food or sleep, drugs, alcohol, smoking, too much television, or associating with the wrong crowd.

Reclaim your heritage today by instituting good habits. When the mind is not pure, meditation can be a challenge, but the after-effect will make you feel more in tune with God. Gradually, as the mind is purified, meditation will not be the battleground; it becomes pure Bliss itself. Physically, mentally, and spiritually feel the spiritual winds of freedom blow gently throughout your entire Being, in tune with Divine Harmony. It is your birth heritage; so why not! Your "hangovers" from now on will be of purity and the Bliss of God.

April 12

MAKING THIS WORLD A HAVEN OF PEACE AND GOODNESS

Yogacharya David, Anandashram, 2005.**

I want to thank those who have kept me in their prayers. This last week we had to postpone Master's Lessons in Bellingham and our Sunday Class on Christian Yoga, times I look forward to and I know others do as well. The reason has been the intense experience God has been putting me through. It is a fact that God carefully censors what I say about such experiences, and I always follow His lead. But perhaps there are a few things I may say about it now.

It is so interesting to explore the "field of consciousness." Even though I live a relative distance from many aspirants, in consciousness there is demonstrably no separation of time or space. Through the all-pervasive Divine Consciousness there is instantaneous and direct connection. Thoughts, feelings, energies, and experiences of others can all be known through God-experience. It is different from a psychic connection, in which a few of the same things may be known. When Divine Consciousness is the medium there is a Supreme Intelligence directing it all, and the Presence of God is constant.

Divine Consciousness makes all the difference. Psychic knowledge alone can create more karma-drama, while Divine Consciousness is uplifting and healing from beginning to end. God can load-share any other person's experiences with me, so I may know their pain, anger, sadness, or compulsions in order to help lift that load and to bring about an evolution in consciousness. This is not something I orchestrate, rather it happens through me. This communion with others is intense and direct.

The reason this does not result in karma-drama is that through Divine Communion, which must be constant, whatever is experienced is instantaneously purified. Through this method, purification can occur for individuals, groups of people, or for larger world conditions.

Each soul is a transmitting and receiving station, and through communion with Divine Consciousness may transmit powerful spiritual vibrations, such as love and light, out to particular souls that come to mind, or various groups, or to creation itself.

The Galilean Master said that there is no greater act than to give your life in service to others, and surely radiating God-consciousness to one and all is a means of fulfilling this sacred duty. As long as you have consciousness, and as long as you commune with the Lord of this universe, then you may be a blessing to one and all by transmitting powerful vibrations of the Supreme Consciousness of God.

Seek always to serve God and each other by first immersing yourself in Divine communion, then let all activity be guided by that inner Source; in this way you will help bring about the transformation of this world to become a haven of peace and goodness for all.

April 16

THE SEED OF AWAKENING

The Tree in Bend, Oregon, where Mother Hamilton meditated.

arly morning hours, long before sunrise, I sit wrapped in the Bliss of God. Thought streams into the conscious mind; it comes whole, complete, and clearly from a Source much greater than my mind. It can come as a complete thought, without words, or it can come as a spontaneous flow of words. It is always fresh, new, even when it concerns concepts I have long entertained. In their newness my understanding grows deeper; it penetrates into the cells and sinews of my Being. I feel a prompting to write down some or all of them. Below are three such thoughts from this morning. By attuning yourself to the spirit of these words you will be lifted up to the same Source from which they have flowed, beyond words or thoughts, into pure Spirit itself.

In winter the tree withdraws into the earth; life becomes "dormant" in the substance from which it originated. Similarly, the yogi withdraws the life-force into the trunk of the spine, and then up the spine until it is reabsorbed back into the original Substance from which he or she has come. Winter ensues in which everything above ground can appear dead, while in reality, the tree is at rest. Then spring awakens the life-energy of the tree, and the yogi, and life flows throughout the organism making it appear to live once again. The tree and the yogi find their natural rhythm in which they rest, are made to exude life back into the organism, flower, bear fruit, and then withdraw back into the ground-substance from which they have come.

Spiritual life tests the aspirant, and through these tests the sadhaka grows stronger. Ultimately every aspiring soul reaches the limit of what he or she can do, and must surrender all effort to Divine Will. Drugs and alcohol on the other hand offer a pseudo comfort that weakens the body and mind, making it dependent on a chemical substance. Rather than passing the test, drug dependence seeks solace in a prison. Free yourself today and boldly walk the earth, moving from victory to victory over limiting forces by becoming a tiger of individual will, and even better, become an instrument of Divine Will.

It can be wonderfully inspiring to read of tremendous mystic feats, such as the human body melting snow in frigid conditions, walking on water, and flying through the air. However, the moment these descriptions divorce you from God, making you think that you must be far away from the Goal, then immediately dispense with all such thoughts. The greatest of yogis will say that such a miraculous event, while true, is not what is essential to spiritual life. Immersing yourself into the Bliss and Light of God is essential for every aspirant. For many, the miraculous appeals to the ego-nature, not to the God-nature. Therefore, miracles are to be avoided due to the tendency of the mind to become sidetracked.

God is dwelling in your heart right in this moment. It is the awakening that has been, and is right now occurring in you, even as a seed awakens while still buried in the ground. While the awakened seed is not yet the great tree it is destined to become, no amount of anxious thought will make it grow faster. Let the dream of becoming the fruit ladened tree grow within you and tend to the needs of the seed right where it is. The miracle of life has already started within you. Water and fertilize the seed with your devotion and by keeping your attention on God. The God-seed within you is destined to stretch its limbs to the Light and merge itself into that self-same Light of God. Victory is assured by ever growing heavenwards.

April 23

UPDATES IN TIDYING

Taj Mahal, India, from the Yamuna River view—architectural poetry.

Before the Wednesday evening class on Master's Lessons there was a general discussion on the effect tidying was having on so many in the room. Not only was there more "clean energy" in the areas done, but the effect on having a clearer consciousness and an ability to focus on getting other things done in life was remarked on by all. There was an air of general excitement at the results being experienced.

This all started when I was talking with an aspirant who had years of frustration at getting a handle on clutter in her house and in her life. We made an agreement to work on de-cluttering our homes and creating last will and testaments as well as living wills for a power of attorney if unable to make decisions for our own medical care. Soon after our agreement, Carla received a recommendation for Marie Kondo's superb book on the *The Life-Changing Magic of Tidying Up*.

While for both this aspirant and I, the tasks agreed upon are still a work in progress, we have both made, and continue to make, significant changes toward the agreed upon goals. The result: we feel encouraged, energized, and it has cleared the way for other projects to move forward that before seemed stuck in the mud.

I know there are some who came into this life with organizing and tidying skills well in place; keeping only those things which give you a spark of joy. For the rest of us, I highly encourage you to try out the methods described in this book; it is life changing.

There are many charming and spiritual aspects to Marie's methods. She comes from Japan and is of the Shinto religion. It is from that perspective she speaks to the individual consciousness that exists in all things. One of her points of view is that everything you have desires to serve you; is in fact anxious to do so. When you put things in the closet and ignore them they are not allowed to fulfill their purpose. When you put them to use or pass them on to someone who will, then they find fulfillment.

Therefore, there is nothing you have that is extraneous; everything has value and a desire to serve. If something has fulfilled its purpose for you, then pass it on and let it serve someone else. If its purpose in this life has been used up, then let it "die" gracefully and with gratitude. Marie points out that the spirit of that thing will then reincarnate as a new item so that it can renew its service to you.

What has become clear is that when your physical space is tidy and clean it manifests in your consciousness as pure energy and clarity. This attitude makes the work of tidying with joy intricately part of your spiritual practice.

April 25

INCREASED ARDOR

Hanuman showing Rama and
Sita in his heart, painting by
Raja Ravi Varma, 1930.**

The impetus to experience God must take on at least the importance of the work you do, money you make, things that you buy, the food that you eat, and the air that you breathe. If you cannot say that it is at least as important as those things, then you have not purified the mind enough.

Pray to the Infinite for Grace so that you are so inspired that you cannot live a moment without the Divine Presence permeating

your entire Being. Find the sweetness of the Divine Name singing itself in your heart, mind, and soul. Practice Kriya Meditation
so deeply that you enter into the eternal Silence of your Soul.
Make the Presence of God so essential that He is with you every
moment of every day. Pierce the veil of separation and see that it is
the Divine Mother's radiance behind the varied masks of creation.
If you feel no urgency for these experiences, if time is passing you
by and you have not a steadily increased ardor for God, then pray
with all that you are for God to awaken Himself within you.

April 28

TURMERIC AND HEALTH UPDATES

Dhanvantari received
Ayruveda from Brahma.

Ever since I have started using the ancient science of oil pulling, taking some oil in the mouth and swishing it about for the recommended time of 20 minutes (I have seen recommendations that span three and a half to twenty minutes), I notice reduced tooth pain and bleeding in the gums, whiter teeth, and an overall good feeling in the mouth. Dr. Fife, a naturopath, has written a good deal on the subject, the importance of oral health, and how it relates to the health of the entire body.

Dr. Fife specifically recommended the use of coconut oil for its anti-bacterial, anti-fungal, and anti-viral punch. Two different people who recently started oil pulling have reported back that when they went to see their dentist, they were told they had the healthiest gums the dentist had seen. Good confirmation for the continued use of oil pulling. Twenty minutes may sound like a long time, but when you combine it with taking a shower, or as I do walking/running on the re-bounder, it easily becomes part of your morning routine. Be sure to spit it out in a trash can and not down the sink as it becomes a solid when less than 76 degrees Fahrenheit (24 degrees Centigrade).

I have also been experimenting with the use of turmeric. Turmeric is used in India's traditional healing arts Ayurveda (life-knowledge). There has been evidence of Ayurveda being used in the Indus Valley dating back 5,000 years. Today turmeric is being investigated in Western medicine for its many wonderful qualities.

Turmeric, with curcumin its active ingredient, is known for being anti-inflammatory (for joint pain among other things), is an antioxidant, leads to better brain health by boosting brain-derived neurotrophic factor, and may lower heart disease, prevent cancer, and help against depression. Turmeric only has about 3 percent curcumin and it is difficult for the body to absorb it (pepper increases its absorbency by 2,000 percent).

I am not good about taking supplements but for the past couple of months I have been using a concentrated dose of turmeric and ginger, adding a couple of pepper corns for absorbency. The result: more joint flexibility and less pain. There are many websites that talk about the benefits of turmeric.[6] One warning is that it is a blood thinner and should not be used if going in for an

---

6   http://authoritynutrition.com/top-10-evidence-based-health-benefits-of-turmeric/

operation. It also must be taken with food or it gives an unpleasant taste when burped up. (Contact your health care professional.)

One of the many uses for turmeric is as a teeth whitener. It helps to produce good oral health (commercial whiteners can actually cause gum inflammation and receding gums). Besides whitening teeth, it is good for sensitive teeth, toothaches, and gingivitis due to its anti-inflammatory, antiseptic, and antibiotic properties, see below.[7] This website includes baking soda in the recipe, which I have not tried as of yet.

A simple recipe is to take ⅛ teaspoon of coconut oil melted, and ¼ teaspoon. turmeric powder in a small cup and mix with your toothbrush (which will be stained yellow), brush onto your teeth and leave for three-and-a-half minutes and rinse. You may or may not notice a difference the first day, but by the third day you will definitely notice whiter teeth; it will also remove stubborn stains over weeks of use.

It is wonderful to find safe, inexpensive, and effective aids for health and well-being, and when I have experimented with them and found them effective, I love passing them on to you. There is much news about the cost of healthcare today, and Western medicine has developed many wonderful treatments. However, I think there are many, many things we can do for our health that are not expensive, that do not require a lawyer or chemist to decipher the warning labels (which sometimes includes death), and that add value to the time that we are in the body.

One of the greats in medicinal history was Hippocrates (400 BC) who is referred to as the "Father of Western Medicine." He is famous today for the oath that all MDs take. He wrote, "Let food be thy medicine and medicine be thy food." He also wrote that "Walking is man's best medicine," Western Medicine would be well served to recall these words, as would we all.

---

7   http://naturalcuresnotmedicine.com/diy-homemade-natural-teeth-whitener/

May 1

A PEEK AT THE RETREAT

Sri Paramhansa Yogananda.**

For those of you who will not be able to attend the Retreat at Loon Lake here is a glimpse of what we will be focused on during our time—an excerpt from Yogananda's commentary on Patanjali. Even if you cannot be there in body, please join us in Spirit.

Krishna told his disciples, "If you don't practice Yoga, you can't attain the final state." Drupada laughed and said, "I admit that, my Lord, but I can't think of anything but

You wherever I look. In order to meditate I have to take my mind away from you." Krishna laughed. "That is the Miruddha state."[8]

Every Yogi must watch his spiritual progress by adjudging the quality of meditation in the following way:

1. Am I continuously restless during meditation racing with likes or dislikes or thoughts? Am I the restless type? Am I restless all the time?

2. Am I so addicted to any good or evil sense habit that when I meditate, I can think of nothing else but that? Am I the mentally obsessed, infatuated type? Am I obsessed by sense pleasures all the time?

3. Am I the type who is momentarily calm and most of the time restless, or am I half the time calm and half the time restless?

4. Am I calm all the time and once in a while restless?

5. Have I attained the last exalted state?

6. Am I fixed in the joy of the soul all the time, unable to be restless anymore?

7. Have I reached the object of meditation—the soul bliss—so that being with it all the time I don't have to meditate on it anymore?

---

8   Quote is from Commentary on Patanjali, by Paramhansa Yogananda, March 8, 1942, sourced from Mother Hamilton's library from her personal copy, found in Yogacharya David's documents on his computer.

8. Has the flower of meditation forever dropped away because the fruit of soul bliss has reached its complete maturity?

The flower precedes the fruit. When the fruit grows the flowers drop away. Meditation is the precursor of soul bliss. When soul bliss is perpetually attained without a moment's separation, then the flower of meditation drops away.

May 5

FROM THE LOON LAKE RETREAT: HITCH YOUR DESIRE TO THE HIGHEST STAR THERE IS

The Star of the Hero, painting by Nicholas Roerich, 1936.**

A sacred feeling resonates in me from the Loon Lake Retreat. The atmosphere was thick with Divine Vibration from dedicated yogis magnetically drawing in higher and higher vibration. There was healing in body, mind, and soul from this charged environment. My only unfulfilled wish is that all could be with us! Of course, you can be there in Spirit, but we like it when you are manifested in body as well!

There is one topic of note that I think you may find very interesting. The Title of the Retreat was, "Does God Have Desire?"

And while we cannot re-enact the entire Retreat here, I will say something about desire nature.

Certainly, it can be said that God has desire when He sets this entire creation into motion. Everywhere about us there is beauty and wonder and awe in beholding what the Creator has accomplished. All evolution of this universe from the coalescence of stars and planets, to the diverse biological species up to humankind, represents a gradual order, splendor, and balance that defies "randomness" of creation.

Enter humankind and you find the expression of desire for survival, satisfaction of pleasures, and expression of self through dominance and structure. In addition to these basic expressions you add creative inventiveness, appreciation of loveliness, caring-ness and compassion. In some, you see only the desire for the basest passions, in others, a nearly unbearable sensitivity for beauty in music, art, and great thought.

The highest expressions of humanity are seen in great spiritual souls; Rama, Krishna, Lao Tzu, Buddha, Christ, and Mohammed, to name a few. Their desire reached across all time and space and touched, nay embodied, Infinity. When seen in the context of little human desires, their desire for Truth, Realization, Bliss, and pure Existence dwarfs anything previously known. These great spiritual luminaries held such an immense desire for God, for Realization, that it could only be fulfilled by an Infinite Consciousness. In evolution, these great ones took desire to a whole new level.

As aspirants, we often find ourselves at war with lower desire nature. The problem from an evolutionary sense is not desire itself, but that we have locked onto little tiny human desires that cannot possibly fulfill the vast desire our Soul has for God-realization; we sell ourselves short.

Rather than curb or kill our desire, hitch it to the highest star there is, Self-realization; not just to the little clods of earthly human desires. Let us expand and intensify our desire until it wants only God. Don't be fooled by cheap imitations but tap into the biggest desire there is. Let us reach out for Satchidananda: pure Being, Consciousness, and Bliss with **all of our heart, strength, mind, and soul!**

May 10

MOTHER'S DAY

Devotees at a Shiva Temple, India, 2005.**

I t is through the Divine Mother that all creation has come into being; without Her, there would be no expression of God. Therefore, we give great homage to the Divine Mother.

Divine Mother is manifest in all women, for they are the embodiment of all that the Divine Mother is. Therefore, we give homage to all women as manifestations of the Divine Mother.

It is because women give birth that we exist as a human race. It is the mother who loves and cares for us through the most fragile and important times of babyhood and childhood. It is our mothers who will love us especially, even as the Divine Mother, whether we are naughty or good. Therefore, we give special homage to our own mother.

And all those who give the love of the Divine Mother to this world can change this world. Ireland was rife with violence for decades until the mothers of Ireland marched in solidarity and said, "No more," and the violence subsided and stopped. The courageous love of mothers is a mighty force.

To the Divine Mother and all Her manifestations here on earth, today we give special honor and recognition to you.

Pronams, I bow to the Light in you.

May 15

Who Are My Brethren?

Birds released from the tiny cage.**

Jesus answered, "Who is my mother? Who are my brethren? . . . Whosoever shall do the will of my Father which is in heaven, the same is my brother, and sister, and mother" (Matthew 12:48–50). In this episode from Jesus' life, he makes it clear that spiritual connection is more important than blood ties.

This can come as a great test for the aspirant; not just with family but also friends, business associates, even with what strangers might think of you if they knew your deep spiritual nature. The fear of what others think, how they might judge you, is a tyrant that never releases you from a self-made prison of what others expect and what judgments they may have.

To free yourself from this prison, you must make what God thinks more important than what others think. There are times and situations that can really test your loyalty to God and to your spiritual path.

One of the things Mother faced, that would be very difficult for many, was when she left for Anandashram in 1957 without any idea of whether she would return or not. Her daughter was pregnant with her first child. As much as Mother loved her children, I can only imagine that this was a pull for her to stay, and that her daughter would have very much wanted her mother there through the pregnancy and after the birth. However, today we are all the great beneficiaries because Mother chose God's direction over familial considerations.

Each of us faces the tyranny of what others think, and in order to have complete union with God we have to make the clear choice for Him alone.

May 19

LOVE AND TRUTH

*Jesus Casting out the Money Changers at
the Temple,* painting by Carl Bloch, 1874.

L ove and truth must go together, or neither can be whole.
There are facts devoid of love, but facts in and of themselves can never be truth. Facts can be used as a weapon to
hurt and destroy, but this is not truth. To know truth, you must
behold not only the facts, but the soul; about which the facts are
but one facet.

For instance, you may know some facts about someone you know, and in anger you throw those facts at the other person without kindness, consideration, or understanding of the entirety of that one, and you may say, "Well, it is only the truth!" But it is not the truth.

When you see the whole person your understanding and compassion grows. You are not focused on a fact, your see the person in the context of who he or she is in the soul's evolution. Inevitably, this leads to love. You may then pronounce facts, but now it has merged with love and it leads to the truth.

When Jesus drove the money changers out of the Temple he was not just in a rage. First of all, he loved God, and he knew so many pilgrims came to the Temple to worship Him as well. All this commerce, shouting out their wares of doves and lambs for sale was not worship, it was changing the feeling of worship into something else. So, it was love for God, love for the pilgrims, and ultimately love for the merchants at the gate; for they were creating karma for which they would have to pay. Jesus was powerfully bringing their attention to this. It was forceful, perhaps even violent, but done with love from beginning to end.

Love is not always meek and mild, but it is always humble; surrendered to God. Be sure before you pronounce something as the "truth" that it has merged with love, for only then does it deserve its name.

May 25

Memorial Memories

Mother Hamilton.

Memorial Day in the United States is a day of honoring ancestors. For many of us, it has not been too many generations since these ancestors were immigrants from far-away places, having left the known for the unknown. These were lives of struggle, sacrifice, and many new starts before getting established. These frontier spirits were really exceptional souls, willing to risk so much for a new life, both for themselves and their future progeny.

On this Memorial Day vintage cemeteries all over the country will have carpets of flowers spread over resting sites of honored ones; stories will be told, quiet memories will bring solemnity, laughter, and sometimes tears. In a world that seems to be always looking forward, today is a time of looking back with love and gratitude.

We are all the products of generations of hopeful lives that brought new generations into life. Today, much is made of dysfunctional families, but by and large families had to be somewhat functional to survive at all. Yes, every family has challenges and patterns that have been destructive, but we also inherit positive qualities as well; this should not be overlooked.

The Ten Commandments tell us to honor both father and mother, for it is in gratitude to these souls that we acknowledge that we have the opportunity for this present incarnation. Our parents made possible our very survival when young. They gave us much of the strength we have, and so many mannerisms and habits are linked to these headwaters from which we have sprung. Even if we are not standing in front of a headstone, we can silently offer flowers of prayerful thankfulness for the good we have received. And then looking forward, be determined to add even greater strength and awareness for ourselves and for future generations.

As a spiritual aspirant, I also look back to the source of grace that has blessed my life. I offer the flowers of my devotion with all love and gratitude as I bow to the feet of my Guru-lineage, as well as realized saints and sages around the world. These valiant souls left known lands to explore vast new realms of spiritual consciousness. These intrepid pioneers gave everything of what they were for this quest, and then went on to produce spiritual progeny to help guide future generations of realized souls.

Each of us has a human heritage, and aspirants for truth have a spiritual heritage as well. Today is a day for giving honor to our human parentage and for our spiritual heritage of Guru, Param-Guru, and Parampara Gurus (great grandfather/grandmother Gurus). In silent gratitude I bow at your feet with all love and humility—continue to bless our lives as I give the flowers of my devotion to you forevermore.

Guru Lineage on altar at Loon Lake, BC.**

May 30

GURU PREM

On the Day of our Lord, I beheld my Guru in her Light body. It had the familiar look of her face and body, but it was all made of a pure white Light, it glowed like the sun shining through crystal glass. From this form a pure white Light shone in every direction, as far as my vision allowed me to see; seemingly into infinite space. With a voice that spoke to my mind she said, "Do you not know, I am in my Light Body now." It settled my mind and I had no more questions, no more doubt. I felt myself to be humble dust at her holy feet. That vision occurred over 30 years ago, and as I recount it, I see it clearly, I feel it profoundly. Who she is is beyond human comprehension!

When I receive some thankfulness from a devotee, I immediately pass it on to her feet; it somehow comes automatically for me to do this. It is through God's inner direction that I write this now, in honor of my Guru. I include below what I wrote in response to just such a note of gratitude I received, and I know it to be the absolute truth. Jai Guru! Victory to the Light ever shining from my Savior-Guru!

> Dearest One,
>
> If there is any good in this form it is all due to our adorable Guru. I would not even want to contemplate what my life would have been without her Divine Presence. All glory to her inimitable life, a Divine Incarnation of inestimable worth to her disciples, to all of this world, and beyond.
>
> Jai Guru, Guru Prem, Ever at Her feet.

Mother Hamilton.

June 4

RECOGNIZING THE DIVINE PRESENCE

Krishna Playing His Flute calling all
back to God, painting by Gargi
(Lakshmi), Anandashram, India.

Recognizing the Presence of God is something many have dif-
ficulty in doing, and doing so consistently. It is not that God
is far away from you, that is not the problem. In fact, for
the brain the opposite is true. The Presence of God is so familiar
that the brain has ceased to cognize it.

Let me give you an example. Your eyes take in photons bouncing off every object in the room in which you sit; however, your

brain has learned to filter out much of what you see as not worth noticing, or another way of saying it, it has become efficient in processing what seems relevant. So, instead of seeing everything in the room within your 180-degree viewing range, your brain only sees certain objects. If someone walks into the room you may notice them only, and while your eyes have been seeing the chair as well as all other objects in the room, they only notice the chair when the person sits on it. The real truth is that what you see is really a complete fabrication by your brain.

All of your senses function in much the same way. Your brain, being efficient, only presents to your conscious mind what it thinks is required and what it can make sense of. If something is not deemed useful, the brain does not see it. There are other faculties of the brain that are also turned on or off depending on what is useful. Your ability to recognize certain sounds, apprecia-tion of beauty, intuition, or God-consciousness are abilities of the brain that may never have been turned on because it was deemed not relevant to your situation.

A spiritually oriented child may never lose the faculty to recog-nize God, while a more earthy child does not see the value in it, so that ability quickly drops away. The Self may be like a breeze you do not notice, or like some fixture in a room you have grown familiar with, or any other countless phenomena going on all around you that you simply do not notice.

In the book, *The Science of Religion,* Yoganandaji makes the point that all human beings seek out happiness, and that only through God-experience can anyone find lasting happiness; there-fore, knowing God is a universal necessity that has been largely unrecognized. When the value of God-experience is truly known, then the search for triggering the part of the brain that can see and feel God begins.

Because the brain is not used to seeing the value in knowing God, it overlooks what it already knows; much like seeing, but not seeing, the chair in the room. Spiritual practice is learning the necessity to know God. Until the brain fully appreciates the value of Bliss, Light, and intuitional Wisdom that can only come from the Divine Presence, it will treat the whole idea like a foreign concept that it chooses not to see or feel.

If your brain does not recognize the supreme value of God-experience, do not think it is because you do not have that ability; rather, slow the mind down, and feel what is already present within you. Learn to perceive the sacred behind all experiences, for it is the vital life within the experience that makes life possible. God is not absent because He is distant; rather, you do not see Him because He is so very close to who and what you really are.

June 12

QUALIFY YOURSELF

The Great Master Mahasaya
and his Divine Romance.

As an aspirant for truth and realization you either qualify or disqualify yourself, based on the purity of your yearning for God. Grace can give you an experience in upliftment, peace, bliss, joy, or some tremendous realization, but this is only the beginning of your journey.

To make continuous progress, you must ever apply the methods a qualified preceptor gives to you. Without this application, the source of Grace will be dammed up, and the flow of spiritual *living waters* will dry up. Without the flow of these living waters, aspiration will evaporate—for without Grace, no real progress can be made.

For every slip and fall on the path, you can trace it back to a falloff of intensity in your spiritual practice. If you find that your practice is dry, that temptation or doubt has crept in the back door and made itself at home in your mind, then let the alarms sound to awaken you to the fact that the liar and thief has made inroads.

Only Light can dispel darkness, only knowledge can dislodge ignorance, and only your sincere desire for God can make you know Him. Make sure you have a love affair with the Infinite, and worship your Heavenly Father-Divine Mother with all of your heart, strength, mind, and soul, and then you will find the sacred Presence a loyal and constant lover that will make you qualified to be an enlightened Being.

June 17

THE MASTER FORGER

Hammer and Anvil with Sparks.**

For durable materials you must use a great deal of heat and sometimes pressure to get a very strong product. And when you are working a metal into a form, you bring it to a forging temperature, about 60 percent of its melting point. The forging temperature allows you to shape the material without creating cracks and weaknesses in it. For instance, the forging temperature for tin is about 450 degrees Fahrenheit (F), while the forging temperature for carbon steel occurs at a whopping 2250 degrees F. If you want to make a very hard substance like a diamond, just like Mother Nature does, then you simply bury carbon dioxide 100 miles deep in the earth, heat it to about 2,200 degrees F, put it under 725,000 pounds per square inch of pressure, and then somehow quickly rush it towards the earth's surface in order to cool.

When man or Mother Nature wants to produce a very hard, durable substance they use these means in order to get the desired results. Mother Nature is not so different, when She is forging character in a human being, and Her masterpiece—causing a spiritual transformation in you.

Divine Mother uses the circumstances in which you are placed in order to create what you are meant to become. In this transformation, you can certainly feel that the heat and pressure are all too much; however, that is because you do not really know what the end product is to be. If the pressure feels like you are buried 100 miles under the earth, and temperatures are soaring to unimaginable heights, then you can only know that what is being produced will be of tremendous strength, hardness, and durability.

Faith in the Master Forger—faith that He knows exactly what He is doing, will give you the endurance to remain in the crucible and take all that He metes out to you. Trust and faith are alloys in your being that allow the transformation to go on with the best results. Surely, your trust and faith will be tested, but that is part of the strengthening and clarifying process you have to undergo. Do not fear. Enter the crucible knowing full well that you are ever under the loving care and watchful eye of the Master Forger.

June 21

SUMMER SOLSTICE

Sunlight through the forest in Northern California.**

Yogis have marked the Summer Solstice with a special reverence for thousands of years. In our modern way of living, we oftentimes become indifferent to the subtle changes in nature, even immune to the change of seasons. The yogis with highly sensitive nervous systems marked these changes, feeling the powerful but refined shifts of vibration throughout the day, seasons, years, and even millennial flux.

Yesterday we gathered in deepened meditation and chanting to avail ourselves of the "thinning" of the veil of separation that occurs during the Solstice. Spiritual skies with a blue vault above and a brilliant Light shining everywhere but with no center revealed itself and made heavenly consciousness an easy reach. Powerful cosmic rays from Divine Consciousness easily flowed from celestial regions. All felt the uplifting forces that purify the whole self.

Today we gather again as these uplifting currents continue to let eagle hearts soar. Join in this dance of the seasons, let joy surge through you as a mighty river, and peace pervade you as an immense sea.

June 26

ALL EXPERIENCE IS WOVEN
INTO THE FABRIC OF YOUR BEING

Yogacharya David viewing the
Ganges, Rudraprayag, India, 2005.**

When you think of letting go of things when they are no longer useful or give you a spark of joy, especially sentimental things, remember that all of your past experiences are already woven into the fabric of your Being. If you were to suddenly leave your home and all of your possessions, taking nothing with you, the life that you have lived, for better or for ill, will go with you even though your hands are empty.

There are things we possess that trigger special feelings, even when you hear a particular song or smell something unique from your past. These sensory cues will bring back a flood of memories and emotions. It is not that the memories are stored as an item, what is heard or smelled; rather, those cues bring forward the memory into the conscious mind, a memory that was always there but residing in subconscious layers of the mind.

The belief that persons or objects are the repository of any particular feeling or thought leads to an attachment that blinds you to an inner reality: whatever you experience already resides within you. Vividly recall any person, place, or thing from your past, and you will experience all the powerful feelings from that time. Then, imagine that situation is no more, and you feel a great and sudden loss. Now imagine that the emotion you experience when you think of a person or place is and has always been within you. When you met someone or visited some place, you may have had feelings that surfaced for the first time, but in reality, those feelings had always been with you.

This is the moral of the story, the story of your existence; all that you treasure, all that you hold dear is right within you, within your heart, mind, and soul. And even if the instruments of body and mind were to become broken or destroyed, your Soul, the repository of your entire existence will forever know those experiences. The love you have experienced, the joy you have known, the security that made you feel whole, all of that and more are elements of who you really are and have always been.

And that is why attachment to things, persons, or the past makes you feel miserable, because you come to believe that you are bereft of those qualities once those conditions have passed. This is an illusion, a wave of the wand of maya, the delusive force of separateness. In God-consciousness, you reclaim all that you truly are, and it is all good. Do not be afraid to let go of those things that tie you to past experiences when it is time to let them go; affirm that you always have them with you, all of that and much, much more.

July 4

LET FREEDOM RING

Fireworks behind the Statue of Liberty.**

Today we in America mark the signing of the Declaration of Independence. While many may not see how revolutionary the ideals set out at the time really were (most the rest of the world simply did not believe this form of government would work). It was a time that set a new course for all people looking to have a just system of rules and government, not just Americans. These ideals have survived many stern tests, and in general have continued on a course of improvement.

No system of government will ever be perfect, for humans are imperfect. However, look to these words set out from the beginning in the Declaration,

We hold these truths to be self-evident, that all men were created equal, that they are endowed by their Creator with certain unalienable Rights, that among these are Life, Liberty and the pursuit of Happiness. That to secure these rights, Governments are instituted among Men, deriving their just powers from the consent of the governed.

By and large these Founders were deeply religious men; many of them were unique thinkers when it came to religion, not at all slaves to the past interpretations. The ideals set out in the Declaration, the Constitution, and the Bill of Rights are all tremendous, and our task has been to bring these ideals to fruition for all people of this country, and that basic, unalienable Rights should be enjoyed by all mankind. And that these rights are not derived from governments, but from God.

Let us all strive to make these words of truth and hope be true for one and all. We might do that by living life as our Creator has wanted us to do. These Founding Fathers were deeply inspired by the teachings of Jesus, and He placed the greatest principles before us. Without the general populace living by such principles, no government will succeed in securing the Rights of all, no matter how lofty the ideas are articulated.

Let us live as Jesus expressed the most fundamental laws of thought and behavior: (Matthew 22:36–40).

Master, which is the great commandment in the law?

Jesus said unto him, Thou shalt love the Lord thy God with all thy heart, and with all thy soul, and with all thy mind.

This is the first and great commandment.

And the second is like unto it, Thou shalt love thy neighbor as thyself.

On these two commandments hang all the law and the prophets.

When we as individuals determine to live in just such a way as spoken by the great Master, then we will enjoy true freedom.

In closing today, I would like to quote from the sage Erma Bombeck:[9]

> You have to love a nation that celebrates its independence every July 4th, not with a parade of guns, tanks, and soldiers who file by the White House in a show of strength and muscle, but with family picnics where kids throw Frisbees, the potato salad gets iffy, and the flies die from happiness. You may think you have overeaten, but it is patriotism.

Let us all think upon the meaning of true freedom today, and enjoy the potato salad before it gets iffy!

P.S. As I just finished this posting, a single eagle flew over the house, gliding on majestically.

---

9   www.goodreads.com

July 13

Best Job—Ever!

Yogacharya David Pronam,
Kausani, India, 2005.**

My first job for pay was cutting asparagus from 4:00 to 7:00 a.m. before school during the spring when I was in the fourth, fifth, and sixth grades; all for 35 cents an hour. Hard physical work was a big part of my life all the way through my twenties. Into my 3rd decade this changed as I entered the fields of counseling and mediation; Mother started this change by asking me to counsel those in the spiritual group and to give spiritual talks for Service.

It's tempting for a "blue collar" kind of a guy to think that helping others to work through the mysteries of the mind or resolving conflicts with others is not really work, but that is looking at it from the outside. Having been on both sides, knowing what hard physical work is, and what hard work it is to be an agent of change, I say that both can be extremely challenging.

Whether it is digging a ditch by hand with a shovel, or working with someone with over a hundred multiple personalities, or doing a neighborhood mediation with six families from a cul-de-sac in conflict, it can all be hard work in different ways. This also has immense satisfaction—in different ways.

In fact, it can seem that the less it looks like work on the outside, the more effort is required on the inside. The theoretical physicist may not look like he or she is doing anything other than daydreaming, but what colossal Causal creations come to mind with single minded concentration.

This could not be truer than when doing spiritual work for myself, or in helping others to do theirs. One can sit in meditation in a half-daze while watching the time, or can exert oneself with all of his or her heart, mind, and soul; think of Master or Mother with tears in their eyes—demanding God to reveal Himself. On the outside there may not be much difference between the two, but one way gets you results and the other does not.

To do this work that God and Gurus have given me is the greatest challenge I can imagine. There is no clocking in or out, the effort and cost is tremendous, but so are the rewards. When an aspirant has worked, and worked, and worked, and finally the results of peace, bliss, and ever-new joy radiate within and without, it is the greatest feeling for him or her, and for me.

The aspirant struggles through every obstacle, often wondering if it will come—will it come? And then the shift comes and it all starts to flow. Like a boat that in lower speeds plows through the water, great effort is required and it makes a big wake, but then suddenly the boat pops up and planes over the surface, same effort or even less, and now it is skimming over the top; it feels like flying! I could not think of anything better than to be a part of this work; there is nothing higher or more fulfilling; in short, it is the best job—ever!

July 18

YOUR LIFE'S NARRATIVE

Ganesha Writing the Mahabharata

Everyone has a narrative about their own lives and its meaning. You can hear it in the stories that are told, the tone and tenor, as well as the content; how those events are selected and interpreted makes up your narrative.

When two people encounter a similar situation, they will each have a unique understanding. An atheist looks out at the world and sees random chaos devoid of higher meaning. A lover of God sees those same events and knows that it is the hand of the Divine that guides every circumstance. Each sees the same event—both have radically different narratives.

I have met those who I have not seen in some time, and they will lead the conversation with, "Let me tell you my latest disaster." In dramatic fashion they will list all the things that have gone wrong in their own lives, or lives of others they know about.

News organizations make it their business to sell bad news, with dramatic interpretations of whatever has occurred, glorifying the salacious, bloody, and tragic in life. Bad news sells, good news—well—doesn't.

We need to be conscious of what we focus our attention upon and on how we interpret events. When Swami Ramdas walked the earth, he saw everything as God, and he was in bliss. When Paramhansa Yogananda looked out upon this creation, he saw the face of God in every flower, tree, mountain, even in a blade of grass. When Jesus stood in front of the supreme temporal power in his world, Pontius Pilate, he declared that Pilate would have no power over him if it had not been given to him from above; in his narrative, he knew that God is the ultimate power.

We love to read about saints and the great epic spiritual stories, whether it is Krishna, Jesus, Hanuman, St. Francis, or Rama. What made each of them heroes is the fact they faced great challenges, but transcended circumstances by keeping their minds upon God alone. Our coming into contact with these heroes awakens the sleeping God that resides in us. Then we take that story and weave it into our own. Our narrative of life takes on new meaning and we see familiar events in life in completely new ways, even as our epic heroes did.

Now we are not merely going to work, but we are in service to God through what we do. We are not just sitting in meditation trying to focus, but we have joined a pantheon of yogis who are merged in a sea of bliss. The obstacles and challenges in our life are not mere irritants, but God testing us to look to Him first, then heroically striving to overcome them. We no longer feel isolated and alone, rather we have a river of love flowing through us to all that we meet; and we feel complete.

It is vital that we get a hold of the narrative of our life. If we leave it to the habits of the past, we will go in circles and arrive back where we started, or be in even a worse condition. But when we conform to the highest Light within, we rise to new heights and join the greatest of realized Beings who have ever lived.

Let's make our life an epic in which Light triumphs over darkness, we discover vast realms of Spirit within, and we are a blessing to all whom we meet—now, that is a story worth telling, and a life worth living!

July 21

FAITH STANDS THE TEST OF REASON

Krishna telling Uddhava: "Satsang–the company of
enlightened ones–helps the devotee to break all attachments,"
painting by Gargi (Lakshmi), Anandashram, India.

An interesting documentary tells how a magician was able to duplicate the feats of Uri Geller (famous entertainer who "psychically" bends spoons, etc.), he also intercepted radio feeds to a healer/minister Peter Popoff from his wife, who was telling him in an earpiece the names and conditions of people who attended his mega-church (attendees turned in cards with names, addresses, and medical conditions they wanted healed when they entered the church).[10] This magician, James Randi, even coached others to fool academics studying psychic abilities (he also, simultaneously, coached the academics to be more rigorous as well, but they oftentimes failed to follow his advice).

This all brought to my mind skeptics of God, the spiritual path itself, and the results claimed by spiritual masters. Let us set aside any claims of the miraculous, which all true spiritual masters minimize, even though we all enjoy stories of extraordinary dimensions concerning God and saints. Instead, we will focus on what is essential to all the great teachings: being established in the true self (which feels to have an eternal nature), to have a clear and expanded consciousness, and to be in a state of mind that is blissful—what in India is called sat-chid-ananda.

Take away the notions of a transcendent God—the simple discovery that individuals have the capacity to experience transformative peace, bliss, and clear consciousness without the use of drugs, alcohol, or other stimulants, is of vast importance. In fact, as reported by all those who attain states of sat-chid-ananda, all other experiences that many people use to find happiness (drugs/alcohol, sex, gambling, etc.), all pale in insignificance by comparison.

Here is the interesting problem for skeptics of God; there is a universal tendency that experiences in sat-chid-ananda make one convinced of a Supreme Being and Consciousness, even if he or she was a skeptic before. In addition, for the attainment of these states of mind, faith in just such a Divine Being accelerates as one enters into this healthy beatific awareness.

For psychologists, sociologists, and anthropologists, there are many studies (from, for example, Michael King of University College, London, from the University of Arizona, and from

---

10   *An Honest Liar.* (2014). Left Turn Films, Pure Mutt Productions and Part2 Filmworks. Directed by Justin Weinstein and Tyler Measom.

Canadian and British Journals of Psychiatry) that speak of the salubrious effect of going to church and having faith in God. For instance, those who regularly attend church report a greater rating of happiness than those who do not; belief in God boosts the immune system, decreases blood pressure, increases life expectancy, and decreases acts of suicide; the more intimate and loving God is perceived, the greater the effect.

This all speaks to the fact that if you want to maximize happiness and health, then believe in God. Regular attendance at spiritual services is a way to reach that goal. Make God more intimate and loving, and you greatly accelerate the outcome.

I was fascinated to watch this debunking documentary; the search for truth is a common ground upon which we can all meet. It offended this magician to see others claiming that what they did could only be done through telekinesis or telepathy, when he could easily duplicate them as a magician. And, when the conditions were properly set to foil a magician's tricks, those claiming higher powers could not perform.

However, I see no substitute for achieving the same results of attaining peace, consciousness, and bliss sans being in a close and loving relationship with God. We need not, nor should we, suspend our reasoning mind when entering our spiritual quest, but happily, reason tells us that faith in a Supreme Being greatly accelerates our attaining the goal of lasting happiness.

July 28

SHADOWS OF DOUBT

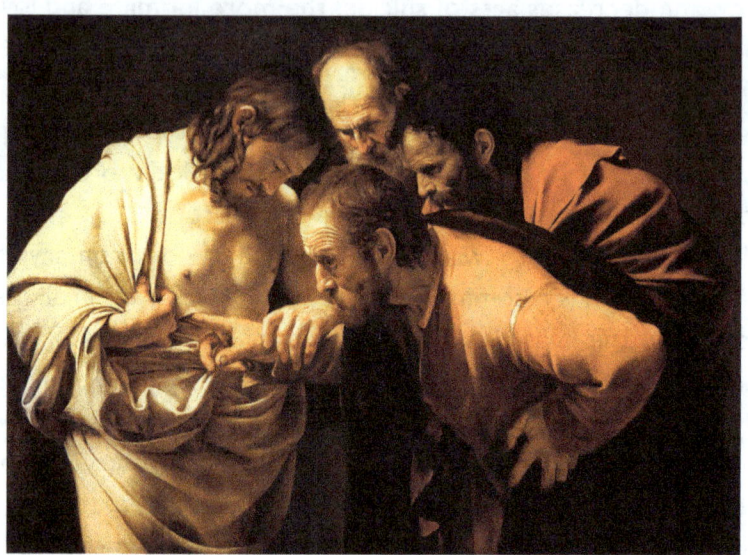

St. Thomas Touching the Wounds of Jesus, painting,
The Incredulity of St. Thomas by Caravaggio, 1602.

There are times in every aspirant's journey when doubt works into the mind and soul. This oppositional force acts with vicious efficiency, wiping out every memory of spiritual enlightenment that had been previously experienced.

These "crisis" moments will come, and depending on what you do with them, they either act to propel you to your goal, or they become a weight that will sink you in a sea of ignorance. Even in the lives of great avatars, storms of doubt railed against them: Rama while in the forest and separated from Sita; Jesus in the garden of Gethsemane; and Buddha during his night of testing.

Doubt in your purpose, doubt in a higher reality, doubt in your teacher/guru, doubt will surround you like a dark, clouded veil.

Through this taxing time, you must recognize it as a test, and despite the lack of light at such a time, faith makes you continue forward. You need not pretend to know anything you do not know, only have faith that the test is a test, and that by remaining loyal to God and guru, you will eventually pass through it.

The path to enlightenment will strip you of everything you know and what you think you know. This empties the cup of the human mind so that you may be born anew in Spirit. When you find that doubt enshrouds you, remember that faith, loyalty, and perseverance are your allies—they will see you through any dark night the soul may encounter. Having traversed this transit of shadows and demons, you will once again merge into light, expansiveness, and a knowing oneness with your beloved Creator—you will once again be your true Self.[11]

---

11   Note: There were no August 2015 Discourses.

September 27

THE BEGINNING OF OUR PILGRIMAGE

Buddha: Jerry and Lois Hickenbottom's home.

Greetings from our Dharmashala on wheels! Carla and I have begun our pilgrimage across this great land. It has been a busy time with events at the house, getting the house ready for our absence, and loading up our home on wheels for an extended voyage. With Ram keeping me in deep inner experiences, as well as a load of physical symptoms, much of the work has fallen on Carla (nothing unusual about that!). Bless her heart.

We ended up leaving on September 23 instead of the 22, and it turned out that this was the actual Autumn Equinox date. This has always been a seminal time of year for me, and this year is no exception. This odyssey came about through God's direction beginning only a month before. After a major change having us purchase a home on Camano Island a little over a year ago, He has now set us off on this extended trip. I had often thought, "If He asked me to leave this beautiful home, I could easily walk out the door without a second thought," and the Divine Creator has taken me at my word!

Our first destination was to Jerry and Lois Hickenbottom in Sunnyside. They have served as Center Leaders for these many years, in addition to having some summer Group gatherings with Lois playing host for several of the children and mothers hosting a craft weekend each year. They too will be moving to Camano Island. A couple were coming to their house to possibly buy it the next day; a closing of a chapter for our spiritual group there as well as the last of our family leaving the Yakima Valley, having arrived over a 120—years before.

Carla and I brought roses from Lois's yard to my parent's graveside in acknowledgment for all they have done to facilitate this incarnation and all their loving efforts for their family. Our hearts welled up with gratitude and love for who and what they are. We also spent time with Cathy, a faithful Kriyaban, and as she watched us depart, she said, "I am the last one to wave goodbye!" And, so it is.

From there we left the known and traveled into the new territory. We crossed the mighty Columbia River, crossed Oregon, and looked to find a place near the Snake River after a long day of driving. Our smart phone was giving us direction to a park to stay when it suddenly refused to give any further instructions. I pulled over after Carla tried repeatedly to get it to cooperate. I tried to renew the connection when a couple came jogging out of their house and asked if we were lost. After hearing our intended destination, they said, "Oh, that is a scuzzy place, you will not want to stay there." Suddenly, she had a phone book in hand that seemed to just materialize, he was calling on his cell phone to check on availability, and with amazing alacrity directed us to a new destination. I was reminded of Steve Fisher's "angels" from his motorcycle trip to Central America. I told them they were our angels come to our rescue. Just as mysteriously as our phone had ceased working minutes before, it now retook its functions with gusto and guided us to a beautiful little park for our stay. Ram, Ram!

The next day brought us to Boise. We wanted to see the campus where Peter's youngest daughter plans to go to college. We rode our bikes on the most beautiful bike trail we have ever been on, following a green belt that is next to a flowing river, crossing back and forth over the river where ducks and geese and white-water kayakers all share the water.

All the while, we continue to organize our sparse 200 square feet of living space. God flows powerfully through this form, and my physical health continues to be difficult, but it allows me to do what is required, and even made me be able to take the 10-mile bike trip, with some breathers along the way.

You continue to be in our thoughts. We feel as if we are taking you with us as we continue on this journey God has put us on for His own inscrutable reasons! Please keep us in your thoughts and prayers, as you will be in ours.

September 30

THE GREAT "I AM"

Sunset at Willard Bay, overlooking the Great Salt Lake.

This writing is sent to you on the anniversary of the birthday of our treasured Lahiri Baba.

A Blood Moon one night and a full moon the next helped mark the anniversary of the Mahasamadhi of Lahiri Mahasaya. On each of these powerful nights, the internal wakeup call comes in what I think of as Sri Yukteswarji's hour, 2 a.m. I open myself to what God would have for me on these nocturnal events, always awake in eager anticipation for fulfilling His will.

My awareness moved out over a vast expanse, like light catapulting from a sun out into vast space. Only this "photon of light" expands and merges into the space into which it is moving, and this "photon" knows unparalleled joy in so doing.

Individuals known to me come to mind, a thousand thousand psychological patterns come into my awareness, clear, and distinct. From the Vedas and from Master's own lips comes the idea, "I am the wave, make me the sea." In the past, I have had a mental image of an ocean, waves rising and falling in natural rhythm, but now it comes as a visionary experience, the sea is a living consciousness. Waves as individual souls emerge from the vast sea of consciousness, each express their unique pattern, then they submerge once again into the vastness of Spirit. This living sea has a number of qualities that defy description: it is full of life—it is smooth and all-powerful; the words are there but they somehow lack sufficient power to convey what it really is.

This great sea is the "I Am," the great "I Am." This "I Am" knows no qualification. It brooks no variance. Anything that needs qualification or change is not the "I Am." Individual waves are always looking for qualifications in creation, not accepting the perfection of it all. Each one has access to the great "I Am," even as the wave stems from the sea, but his or her insistence on qualifications keeps him or her from merging into the sea.

The perfectness of the great "I Am" cannot be compared to anything—for it is unique perfection itself. These are the writings of a madman; mad for God, mad in God-experience. I have had to break the tethers of the known in order to chart these waters of the unknown. Having done so, I am now commanded by the same Intelligence that guides this exploration to write down these notes from beyond the Beyond.

I can tell you beloved friend, the great "I Am" answers all of the heart's desires, it fulfills the soul with its constant restless tides, and it is easily accessible by all. Oh, my dear ones, simply make no qualification upon God or His creation, humbly accept everything in its perfection, merge into the great "I Am," and join Lahiri Baba and the great ones in knowing this fathomless Truth of your Being.

I am now emptied of what I held within from this experience, giving it all to you, and I merge into the great "I Am," merging into what I never left and what will always be mine, even as it is yours.

October 4

SALT LAKE CITY

Salt Lake City Cathedral.

Our pilgrimage continues. Corliss had recommended that we camp near Thousand Springs Falls, Idaho. Ninety miles away, a river dives subterranean into lava tubes and travels underground until it finally emerges from the midst of a cliff face and drops down to join the Snake River below. It is a beautiful oasis in the midst of desert; an excellent tip for an overnight stay.

Our next stop was Shoshone Falls. Taller than Niagara Falls, the rock formations formed by the fluidic master engraver are really breathtaking. We pilgrims took our time to imbibe the special feeling of peace and vital energy while there. From there, we traveled south into Utah. Our new "home" came close to the Great Salt Lake at Willard Bay State Park. The park, mostly empty this time of year, was a welcome respite and provided a peaceful haven in which to stay with a rich population of birds and expansive views of the unique Salt Lake.

Then on to Salt Lake City. Settled by the Mormons, I had wanted to visit the holy sites that drew these intrepid pioneers. Establishing a Temple for the living God was an important mission for the Church of Jesus Christ of Latter Day Saints. Brigham Young said he did not like to say too much about the revelations he received from God, but he definitely felt the Spirit of God was present where he said the Temple should be built.

Through much hardship the settlers not only worked to eke out a living but also donated their time for 40 years in order to complete the Temple. Using quarry rock from 20 miles away, the granite stones were at first hauled by wagon, later by a railroad system that was built to accomplish the task. Truly, a beautiful Temple was constructed and the manicured grounds surrounding the Temple have a very peaceful feeling to them.

We were also treated to an organ recital at the Mormon Tabernacle with its amazing sound acoustics beautifully engineered into the oval roofed structure featuring the biggest organ I have ever seen. It was wonderful. A local recommended we eat at the Red Iguana, a Mexican restaurant. We were treated to the most delicious tacos ever. The tightly packed tables and noisy ambience reminded me of Yogi Berra's (yes, the Yankee catcher was named after Hindu yogis!) comment, "Well, no wonder nobody eats here, it's so darn crowded!" But the taste of those delicious tacos stays with us still.

Carla had made me promise that if certain physical symptoms continued by the time we had arrived at the city, then I would see a doctor here. Frequent shortness of breath, pounding heart, dizziness, and lack of physical energy have been my constant companions these past months; making it an act of will to do the simplest of activities. The doctor saw me at the University

Walk-in Clinic. Both an allopathic and a Chinese medicine doctor, she tested me for blood pressure, checked heart and lungs, as well as oxygen intake, etc. I tested out perfectly in all categories. The doctor was perplexed by my symptoms and apparent perfect health. She asked if I would be open to some Chinese formulas for breathing and dizziness. I have been taking them for the last couple of days, so far, without noticeable effect.

One of the legacies of receiving Mother's Spiritual Mantle has been the taking on of every form of ailment and psychological condition from others. The Grace that goes with this work that I do for Mother is that I know God's Presence from beginning to end. This makes all the difference. It does not mean that I do not meet with frustration at times, or feel that what He is giving me is too much, but these are passing phases—I would not trade my life for any other.

When I leave on a pilgrimage trek I smile when someone says, "Have a nice vacation." I appreciate the sentiment, but there is never a time God does not have me at work. This life I live I find fascinating, even as a spectator of a sporting event would find the play on the field fully engaging.

We left Salt Lake City feeling that we had an opportunity to experience the holy sites. Carla said that it was the cleanest city she had ever been in; I told her it rivaled Singapore in that respect. The people were all friendly and the emphasis on a healthy family was evident. It is wonderful to come to a city where the Temple is the center attraction.

As we traveled south, we were surprised at the dense population that continued past the city proper. Eventually, we felt the relief of leaving the dense population and felt the open skies unfurling before us. We are now stationed at Yuba State Park, looking out over Yuba Lake. The soft colors of desert hills charm us, then as the sun sets a vibrant thunder and lightning storm passes nearby. We are thankful for our dry dharmashala on wheels and all the comforts of home (in miniature). This morning the early morning skies herald the rising sun with trumpets of orange, gold, and blue colors streaking overhead.

Note: We recently received word that Sheela (of Prem and Sheela) has left the body. Sheela had been having health problems for some time. We always remember Sheela for opening her San Diego home to all of us so freely and lovingly, delicious meals and their Thursday night kirtans. Sheela had a wonderful sense of humor and was totally devoted to Prem (Papa Ramdas' grandson), Papa, Mataji, and Swamiji. I always remember her saying as she lovingly looked upon her husband Prem, "The only thing harder than being a saint is living with one!" I am sure that they were all there for her transition into her new life, now free in joyful Spirit. Om Sri Ram Jai Ram Jai Jai Ram!

Carla and I both pass on our loving thoughts to you and may God and the Masters ever bless you.

October 8

The Sculptures of Arches National Park

Arches National Park, view from our
camping spot on the Colorado River.

A pilgrimage can hold many different types of adventures. The common thread in the weave of a pilgrimage is the sacred nature of the journey. After leaving Yuba Lake south of Salt Lake City we climbed and climbed until we motored over a pass that was nearly 8,000 feet above sea level; instead of being covered with trees, it was desert sage and rocks. We descended to Green Lake, and the next morning we were on to the town of Moab, located close to Arches and Canyonlands National Parks.

We had planned on meeting Rick and Judy in or around Moab but without naming a specific time or place. Carla and I followed the road up the Colorado River where there were some camping sites dotting the river. Passing one campground after another with each one showing full, we finally came to one that had just a couple of very nice sites open next to the river. We selected what we thought was the best one for us and started to set up camp when Rick and Judy pulled in and took the site next to us, the only one in the campground that could have accommodated their larger fifth wheel trailer, and the only one of two left along the entire canyon. Judy had just been commenting to Rick that they had lost their phone connection in the deep canyon and how would they ever find us since they were now miles from Moab. And then they recognized our Bigfoot motorhome, and a free campsite next to us; it brought tears to her eyes! God arranged everything without cell phones, through a much more reliable and secure form of communication than humans ever invented—His loving Divine care and sure guidance!

Although the Temple at Salt Lake City was a definite interest of mine to experience, the real draw for me from the beginning was to be in nature's cathedrals of expansive desert. Today we entered into the unique geography of Arches National Park. Over millions of years a salt bed was laid down by a shallow sea filling the area and then drying up. This repeated filling up and drying out built up an immense layer of salt. Through plate tectonic motion the earth rose, and the salt, now under layers of sandstone rock, bulged up, then the rains dissolved the underlying salt which collapsed the earth in this area. This collapse stretched the surface layers of sandstone that made them spread and crack. Now rain mixed with carbon which made for an acidic combination sculpted the sandstone into the most unusual shapes.

Upon entering the park, it was clear that we were in a most fantastical place. Columned towers, great walls rising up hundreds of feet and stretching for many miles, great round rocks balanced on narrow tall pedestals; there seemed to be no bar to the creation of every fantastic shape you can imagine by the master Sculptor who used sandstone as his medium, and acidic rain and wind as His carving tools. We drove 18 miles to the end of the road, a place called Devil's Garden and walked the path toward the many red sandstones shapes.

Although I was easily winded by the small hills, I was able to walk further than at any time in the past weeks. Earlier my physical health had seemed to take a dire turn, I had no coloring and Carla was very concerned. Inwardly, I felt that I could give up the body at any moment. However, I had a stern talk with God and told Him it would be very wrong to take me now and leave Carla with the RV and to have to handle all arrangements for this body in such a remote location as we were in at the time. I told Him under no circumstance should He put her into that situation. Thankfully He did not.

We continued our way back through the park and drove by natural sculptures, and with very little imagination one reminded me of Horus, the Egyptian bird, another of the Egyptian Sphinx, and yet another of the face and body of an immense serpent in an area called the Garden of Eden, and then there was a stone in the shape of the Buddha. As we drove on immense sentinel warriors rose hundreds of feet high to stand guard. Striking pillars fit for the palace of any king or a temple to God were everywhere, only multiplied by many dimensions; all of them colossal, dwarfing our human tiny attempts at art or architecture. Art was etched into the walls of these mighty corridors. It seemed that all human effort at creation has been anticipated by the Creator in this marvelous setting.

Finally, we came to a stop at the Fiery Furnace. The bright red sandstone reached up in columns that could remind someone of flames leaping up. However, this place was both physically and energetically a cooling place. As we sat in its midst, a great sense of peace and calm came to me. Ah, this is the pilgrimage spot to which Divine Mother had brought us. From here we could look out over a vast panorama of sculpted shapes dotting the land-scape below, in the eastern distance high snowcapped mountains in the state of Colorado rose up on the horizon. It was a surpass-ingly lovely view and the Fiery Furnace brought the gift of awak-ened spiritual energies. It is a pilgrimage spot chosen for us by Prakriti's Mother Nature.

And now, as I write this to you, we sit next to the Colorado River in a deep ravine with red rock cliffs soaring above and jag-ged peaks all around us. The campfire is burning, the vivid stars are shinning, gentle rapids next to us sing their continual song, and we are serenaded by the crickets living nearby. A wonderful sense of peace like a warm blanket, settles around me as I think of you—separated by distance, but not in Spirit.

So, I send to you this gentle peace, the peace I felt at the Fiery Furnace (perhaps it is misnamed) here by the lapping waves of the Colorado, and I am filled with gratitude for God guiding us so perfectly and truly in this pilgrimage of His natural wonders.

Yogacharya David and Carla at the Fiery Furnace.

October 10

Mt. Vernon Dharmashala

Mt. Vernon Dharmashala.

Adharmashala is a shelter dedicated to right action or holiness. When Carla and I were able to purchase the Mt. Vernon house we definitely wanted to dedicate it as a place of right action, and to make it a place where, through deepened meditation and activities for the spiritual group, it became a place of holiness as well.

When we first drove by and saw the For Sale sign, I stepped out of the car, loved the feeling of the land, and very much liked the Cape Cod style of the house. "Wouldn't it be wonderful to be able to buy this home," was the wistful thought we both had. At the moment there was no associated thought that this would be something we would ever be able to do.

Somehow, through some fairly miraculous and timely circumstances that unfolded a step at a time, we were allowed to eventually buy that very house we so circumstantially happened to drive by. However, buying the house was only the beginning of the adventure. The house had been built in 1950, and while it had been greatly loved by the Fishers, who had lived in the house for 50 years, it held much promise for many improvements.

From the beginning, George and Christine gave so lovingly of their time, energy, expertise, and financial support to make improvements on the house. I hesitate to mention the many helpers for fear of leaving anyone out, but Greg, Larry, Herlwyn, Bruce, Janice, Peter, Brad (and Sparky), Dianne, Andrew, Cate and Charmie all come to mind for giving of their time, labor, and in many instances money as well for bringing the Mt. Vernon Dharmashala into a much higher expression of beauty and grace for all to enjoy.

Besides those who came for painting parties and working on the landscaping, there are those who came to meditate and pray. The number of Silent Saturdays with deepened meditation, the Services, Christmases, and Easters, the baby and wedding showers, the guests who came to do their spiritual work, all combined to create a spiritually charged environment. The house hummed and shined with intense spiritual vibration that grew with each passing year.

Now, 10 years have amazingly passed by since we first stepped out onto the land and felt the wonderful vibration of the many cedar trees and the ground itself. I pray that each person who contributed to making this home a true dharmashala receive much in return for all that has been given. No words can express our feeling of gratitude and the deep mystery of what can happen when many willing, loving hands come together to create something beautiful for God.

It is time to pass this beautiful creation on to a family who will both benefit from, and add to, the feeling and beauty this home has been created with. In thinking of putting this home up for sale my thought has been, "May the right family be drawn to this house and fill it with new happiness, holiness, and find fulfillment here; be this for the highest good of all!"

After writing the above, we received word that we had two offers in the works, and the first offer was upped to a full price offer after seven days on the market. I cannot help but think that the feeling/vibration of the house from all the spiritual work done there added to the appeal of the home.

Note: I went in for blood tests here at the Moab Family Clinic on Friday and will find out the results on Monday. I always offer a complicated medical picture as the internal experiences have "physical features," so knowing what is physical, and what is spiritual, can be difficult to differentiate. I do feel this shortness of breath, and at least some of the fatigue, is a result of something physical which has prompted the further testing. We will keep you informed.

October 17

BENDING AND RE-SHAPING REALITY

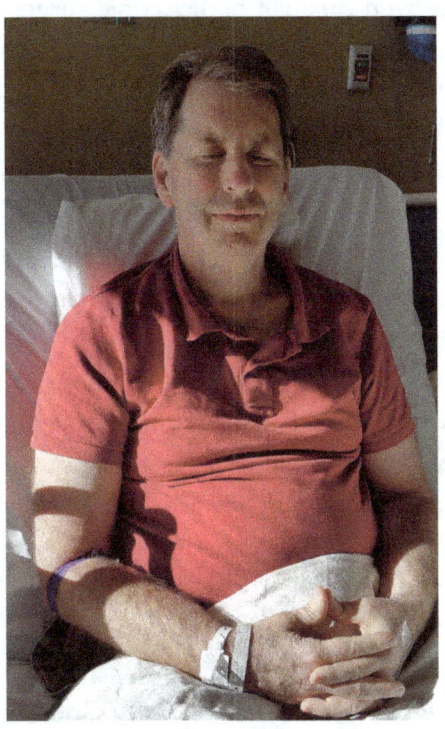

Yogacharya David communing
with God in the hospital.

Early morning reveries are a common way that God reveals His more subtle and profound Truths to me. In the darkness the world is quiet and His whispered thoughts come unbidden, but not unwelcomed.

This morning God was telling me about bending or re-shaping reality. He used the example of this last week's events of going into the hospital. From Monday morning we were told by the emergency room doctor and the colon specialist that in all likelihood I had cancer. After the colonoscopy the specialist was certain that I had cancer, even though he said he could be wrong. Even if I did not have cancer, I would still need to have a portion of my colon removed through orthoscopic surgery.

Fast forward to getting the biopsy reports. The same doctor now said that not only would I not need surgery, but that he felt he destroyed the non-malignant tumor. Although quite large, over a centimeter, he removed some of it and cauterized the rest. He recommended a couple of follow-up tests, but they could wait.

From the certainty of an operation and the high probability of cancer to, "You will need no further treatment at this time," was a very big change of reality.

God explained this morning. The number of prayers being issued by powerful souls had bent and reshaped reality. In the experience, God showed me prayers being put forward by high-souled individuals, I saw with inward vision the effects of those prayers changing this medical situation.

This was not some vague idea or thought of, "That is how it should work," rather it was a reality I was experiencing. It was fascinating to see the entire process from His perspective. The greater connection the individual has with God, the more focused the mind, the more powerful the prayer. Each individual's prayer varied in strength, but every one of them counted and had its effect.

The doctors and nurses and hospital staff certainly played their essential roles, and overall, I was very impressed with the treatment I received there. However, there was also a powerful hidden force at work—your prayers. It is with profound gratitude that I thank you for those prayers and the love that went behind them, and the fact that God has given us each other so that we might make this journey together back to Him.

I know from my own experience that deepened prayer brings me closer to God and thus acts as a blessing to the one praying. Whether it is an individual, or dozens, hundreds, thousands or millions, prayer has the capacity to bend and re-shape reality in positive ways. One person, close to God, may have a greater effect than millions, but no prayer is lost or insignificant in the eyes of the Lord. Let each one of us deepen our communion with the Infinite and therefore be a greater conduit for His blessings going out to this creation.

October 21

FROM MOAB TO BRYCE

Rick and Judy Ellis with Carla and
Yogacharya David: River Boat Ride.

With a gradual recovery of my health taking hold, Carla and I set up an evening boat ride on the Colorado River with Rick and Judy as a thank you for all the support they provided while I was out of commission; Rick helping Carla with the RV, Judy by making delicious meals for us, and the use of their pick-up to run the many errands required.

The boat ride started with dinner in a banquet hall next to the Colorado River at dusk. Tall older men in cowboy hats greeted us with friendly Western hospitality, then we had a lovely meal and then onto the jet boat that held 140 people in rows of seats. We had some earlier rain but not a drop all through the boat ride. As we gently made our way upriver we received a geology lesson by our entertaining guide; he also pointed out an immense stone crocodile, images of fish on the cliffside, he said it was a rockfish, and several visages, one looking like W.C. Fields.

Making the turn to go back down river we were accompanied by a land vehicle that had enormous lights that lit up the canyon walls as the history of creation from the Bible was told. And for all appearances, the face of God seemed to be looking out from the rock face as it was brilliantly lit. The history of the native peoples in the area as well as early pioneers and desperadoes was described as we gently floated downstream. All in all, it was an entertaining and unique view of the canyon.

In the morning, we broke camp and made our way toward Fruita, now a state park, once the site of a small settlement of a few intrepid families. Located in a narrow valley of red rock, a small river made it possible for early native peoples and later pioneers to plant crops and supplement game for their living. The early native peoples preceded the Hopis, whom the Hopis called the ancient ones. For some unknown reason they left the area. Next came a Mormon settlement of a few families. They planted orchards and supplemental crops and lived by bartering their goods for grain and other essentials. By WWII they too left the area.

This was a charming little valley, but after a night's stay it was clear that the cottonwoods were causing allergic reactions for Carla and we left it. Having been separated from Rick and Judy in Moab, Carla and I headed out to places unknown. One of the great things about a motorhome, if where you are does not suit you, then you simply fire up the engine, and off you go to better places.

We traveled on to Escalante and found a lovely state park in which to stay overnight. In the a.m. we were on to further places unknown. A thought we had earlier was to go to Bryce Canyon, but the weather was rainy and cool and the altitude there is very high. However, as the highway brought us near to the National Park we felt a pull to enter in.

We climbed up to 8,000–9,000 feet in altitude and were immediately charmed by the locale. The long needle pine trees and rocky terrain reminded us of Dronagiri in India where Babaji initiated Lahiri Mahasaya. Carla's allergies were clearing in the mountain air and we found a lovely spot in which to camp. We drove the two-lane road to see one magnificent vista after another. Not so much a canyon as a series of amphitheaters, Bryce seems to be created to delight and astound its viewers.

No artist has ever had a palette filled with such colors. Oranges, reds, and golds are magnificently vibrant with varying shades and hues, but all the colors are intense and rich. Hoodoos rise up from the height of a man and on up to 150 feet tall with varying thickness layer after layer, like a totem pole. While there is nothing specifically spiritual in these cliff formations, their eye-catching beauty and chiseled looks inspire the mind to appreciate what Mother Nature can do. Quite often either Carla or I will automatically and quietly proclaim, "Oh God Beautiful!"

The combination of thinking of Babaji, the feeling of clean air, and the remarkable beauty that lies outside our door, makes us think we will tolerate the periodic rain showers and the cold nights for a while longer. That, and this weekend is predicted to be filled with sun.

Being in Nature's Cathedrals is a big part of what drew me to this part of the world. Here at Bryce National Park, I feel a wonderful fulfillment in the feel of clean energy and abundant beauty that God meant for us to experience on this pilgrimage.

Hoodoos at Bryce National Park.

October 25

TIME PASSAGES AT BRYCE NATIONAL PARK

Bryce National Park, view of Hoodoos.

Pilgrimages have a way of condensing time. Each time I have gone to India on pilgrimage, it seems that the intensity of experience makes it seem that it must have been far more time than what the calendar says. After a month on this pilgrimage Carla and I looked at each other and we both said it seems more like a year than a month!

This is not just because it has been difficult or painful, which can also condense time, for we have had so many extraordinary experiences in nature that have been wonderful. Even now, we continue our stay at Bryce National Park. We live in a forest of Ponderosa Pine, just steps away we can walk to the canyon's edge and be witnesses to one of nature's great sculptural masterpieces, breathe remarkably pure air at over 8,000 feet, and as of the last couple of days, we have deep blue skies above. No, it just seems a very long time ago since we left on this journey.

We have explored the series of "amphitheaters" that make up Bryce Canyon, each one with different characteristics and individual charms. We can only imagine how crowded it must be in summer months, but now there is a steady trickle of fellow gawkers, many of them northern Europeans of various nationalities. There are hikers and mountain bikers, and the look, click, and dash folks (they race to the view point, look, click some pictures and dash off to the next view as if some invisible timekeeper will award them a prize for being the fastest tourist of the day!).

We tend to move slowly, some of that is dictated by this body, but it is also a desire not only to look, but to feel on a deeper, intuitional level. These canyons are not static, but in a sense, living. Through erosion they are constantly changing, only their life cycle occurs over tens and hundreds of thousands of years. One of the Indian legends says that there were people living here long ago and they became evil. The prankster coyote turned these evil people to stone, and if you look at the Hoodoo formations you can still make out their faces in the rock.

When you listen deeply, there is a great quiet and purity. Although we have no schedule it seems we have spent extra time here; it has been good for the healing of this body as well. We will be moving on to other places soon, but other than the cold (there are over 200 days a year that have freezing temperatures and we have been here for a few of them), it has been a wonderful time.

It is always interesting to see the world through what others perceive. Ebenezer and Mary Bryce were homesteaders whose backyard was these magnificent canyons and for whom the park was named. When Ebenezer was asked what he thought about these canyons that eventually became a National Park, and where millions of visitors would come to take in the views, he thought about it for a little while, and said, "Well, it's a helluva place to lose a cow." Well, Ebenezer, I am sure it was!

Health Note: I continue to be able to do more each day, although it is slower than I would like. I was having a constant burning pain in my stomach, so on the advice of the insurance nurse over the phone we drove a couple of hours to a walk-in clinic. The doctor there prescribed some antibiotics for a stomach ulcer (it is only the third time I have had antibiotics). It has been a couple of days, but I am noticing improvement. The doctor in Moab suspected I might have a stomach ulcer. It was only recently that an Australian researcher announced certain types of ulcers were caused by bacterial infections. He was ignored and scoffed at by the medical establishment until the evidence convinced a reluctant institution. Today I am getting treatment based on his tenacity to go forward in the face of ridicule by "the experts."

Additional Note: October 24 is the second anniversary of Christine leaving the body. She continues to feel very close to me. We were in India on pilgrimage two years ago when we received word that she had left the body. We had a laminated picture of Christine and took it to every holy place we went and dipped it in the Ganges when at Ma's ashram. Although the outcome was not her complete physical recovery as we had hoped deep in our hearts, she did have a most glorious leaving of the body and left as a freed soul. The day before her 2nd anniversary I spontaneously bought some lime-flavored Tostitos, a product I have never bought before. On the day of her anniversary, I took the bag out and opened it and Carla said, "Christine always bought those when she came down, they were her favorite and she couldn't get them in Canada!" So, we ate some Lime Tostitos at Rainbow Point here at Bryce in memory of our sweet Christine.

October 29

SOMETHING IS TERRIBLY WRONG HERE

The physical dimension is only one aspect to a pilgrimage. For one who has attunement to the inner senses, there are many more ways of perceiving this world we live in. As we were traveling in Southern Utah, we heard many stories of how Brigham Young had "ordered" particular families to come to specific areas to make their homes.

Many of these places proved not to be conducive to successful communities for a variety of reasons: weather, poor land or a native population that was not in favor of having new neighbors. As I continued to hear these stories, an oppressive feeling came over me about this dynamic, and I felt a soul sickness within— something felt terribly wrong here.

I must say I have been around, and known Mormons, most of my life, and I have a highly favorable opinion about most all the folks I know. But this oppressive, painful experience continued to grow as we traveled west. It came to a head when Carla was reading about an event known as the Mountain Meadow Massacre; we happened to be right in the area it occurred.

The Mountain Meadow Massacre took place September 11, 1857 at the time of Brigham Young and the church's desire to settle Utah Territory for Mormons was at its height. Young had become more strident in his call for making this area a place for Mormons only. Meanwhile, a comparatively wealthy group of pioneers from Arkansas with a large herd of cattle were travelling south in Utah going to California. When the group was in Salt Lake City, they were refused re-supply because they were not Mormon, so they were struggling just to make it out of the territory.

A local militia group of Mormons dressed up as Indians attacked these settlers, probably hoping to steal their cattle. They were recognized as being whites, not Indians, and so they made a terrible decision to cover up the truth. A group of Mormons under a white flag approached the travelers who had been under siege by the "Indians" for five days. The Mormons said they could help the Arkansas pioneers get through the dangerous Indian Territory. The pioneers agreed and allowed themselves to be led into an ambush by the rest of the group and every man, woman, and child was killed; one hundred and twenty souls. The only exceptions were those younger than seven, and they were adopted into Mormon Families by the very people who murdered their families and stole their belongings. They were just 40 miles from entering California.

There is a long story in all of this. However, a Mormon investigator, in the end, found blame in the murderers' greed, and in the increasingly fiery talk from Brigham Young about the area being only for Mormons. When Carla read this to me, it fit exactly the overwhelming feeling I had been having, and my discomfort with families ordered here and there by the church hierarchy for the purpose of establishing a territorial claim. Eventually, the children incorporated into the Mormon families were found and an effort was made to reunite them with their families in Arkansas.

This is a strange story, that something that happened so many years before was felt so strongly by me now without my having any pre-knowledge of these events. It highlights the fact that whatever is done *cannot be done in secret*, and it *shall be shouted from the rooftops*. I have a strong feeling of grief for those innocent travelers and for the terror they went through. I have hesitated in writing this as part of this pilgrimage, but when I awoke this morning, I found the story being written in my mind and a strong prompting to make this part of our record.

As we continued our travels, these intuitive feelings of grief have remained but with less intensity. We motored from the lovely

Bryce to Zion Canyon. One thing that is very interesting is how different each of these National Parks has been. We entered Zion from the east entrance and marveled at the strange rock formations there, looking like upside-down beehives hundreds of feet tall. We then went through a couple of tunnels, one of them over a mile long with occasional "windows" looking out over steep drop-offs. We then emerged into the south part of the park.

Yogacharya David and Carla at Temple of Sinawava, Zion.

The weather is warmer here, not freezing at night, and we have found ourselves at a lovely campground near the south entrance. We hiked up the trail where the road stops at the canyon's end called the Temple of Sinawava; we were in awe of the steep cliffs on both sides that eventually narrows to a few feet wide as you proceed up the Virgin River. On another day we drove to Kolob National Park and took a hike to its vistas. Superlatives simply have to give way to silence, for there seems to be one magnificent view after another on this pilgrimage—too many to describe. We continue to enjoy each and every day and look forward to what God will bring to us next.

Health Note: I continue to grow stronger, although each day varies in what I can do and how fast. My blood count has remained steady but below normal, and I have now finished the antibiotics for the stomach; there has been overall improvement. My health seems to be on the right track, just slower progress than I would like. I will now work to improve my stomach health with probiotics.

October 31

DIVINE MOTHER AND ALL
SAINTS EVE/DAY AT ZION PARK

Yogacharya David meditating in Zion Park.

t is very interesting to notice not only the physical surroundings you are in, but also the subtle vibrational reality that accompanies all creation. Spiritual beauty and physical attractiveness can be at complete variance with one another, and then on some occasions they express themselves equally through some charming form as in the case of Mother Hamilton.

Without doubt, Bryce Canyon is breathtakingly magnificent in its vistas with colors that seem from another world. When we arrived at Zion Canyon, we found it visually stunning as well, but not on the same order as Bryce. However, we have found Zion to have a spiritual power that was often not felt at Bryce; the exception at Bryce was Fairyland Canyon, which had a wonderful, spiritually uplifting feeling to it.

Before arriving at Zion, we passed through the most vibrationally painful area where the Mountain Meadow Massacre occurred (see previous posting). That ungrieved-for tragedy that happened so long ago continued to envelop us as we entered Zion Park.

After finding a campsite near the south entrance, we took the motorhome back up the road near where the tunnel exits. We hiked up the canyon along a sweet creek, climbing around boulders following a faint trail that led us into the canyon's wilderness. At last, we came to a spot where the trail crossed the creek and decided to sit for a while, feeling drawn to meditate there. Turning our attention inward also made us more aware of the powerful spiritual current flowing in that spot. Divine Mother had drawn us here in order to baptize us in her holy vibrations.

We felt washed clean of the pain that we had carried from the massacre site as we allowed those invisible healing "waters" to flow around us and through us. It was unspoken by either of us until afterward, but we both reported identical experiences while there. Such is the wonderful healing potency that comes with pure nature. It seems that the earth has natural places of healing, and then there are places surcharged by saints and souls of great realization, and then there are places that have both of these blessings combined. Being next to that creek was simply one of Mother Nature's natural healing gifts.

Today we found another such place. In this case the location is much more public. A set of immense cliffs are the backdrop to the museum here at Zion. Obviously, these towering edifices made by water's power and sculpting methods also inspired early settlers, for they named this place Temples and Towers. Here you will find peaks called the West Temple and the Altar of Sacrifice.

After touring the visitor center, we happened upon the rear entrance and happily discovered the most imposing scene.

We were both instantly enthralled by the dramatic cliffs and peaks we saw. It was not just the visual delight of the view, but the definite feeling of spiritual power emanating from these craggy heights. We both sat and entered stillness at the behest of this Temple of Nature. How long we sat is hard to gauge, perhaps not long, perhaps it stretched out into eternity. Different visitors came and went as we remained, emphasizing the vastness in time of this mountainous creation, making it seem that humans were just tiny fly-like visitors flitting in and out, barely noticed by these geologic patriarchs.

Both of these healing, uplifting gifts of nature came to us unbidden and without any pre-knowledge by us of their coming. Perhaps Divine Mother delights in surprising her children with these blessings of Spirit that uplift and heal Her very own.

As we greet All-Saints Eve today, honoring all saints known and unknown, we can readily identify so many saints that were inspired by nature's spiritually-charged environments. Babaji, Jesus, and St. Francis come to mind in thinking of their love and reverence for the spiritual nature of creation; its beauty and wonder. It is in the spirit of Divine Mother's recent gifts to us, that have been so freely given, that I pass on to you all of their uplifting and purifying power even as we felt it, for you to feel Her blessings on this All-Saints Eve and coming Day.

November 6

From Snow Canyon to Valley of Fire

Snow Canyon from North Galoot.

From Zion National Park we toured our way toward St. George, on the Utah-Arizona border. Rick and Judy secured a camp spot for us at Snow Canyon State Campground just north of St. George. It is a beautiful campground in a valley of red rock formations that was discovered by white settlers when they looked for some lost cows in the area. There is evidence that native people were inhabitants thousands of years before that.

We took a hike up the Lost Pinion Trail that took us through narrow cracks between rocks that opened into small meadows of beautiful, soft, green sage plants unlike I have ever seen before. Another day took us on foot up to the North Galoot with vistas in every direction. While I struggled for breath at times, I went on every hike and climbed every peak I set my sights on. The quiet nature of the park and the large distances between campsites made this stay a favorite for Carla and me.

We took a day to tour Brigham Young's winter home in St. George and to view the large Mormon Cathedral (the first Mormon Cathedral in Utah). I had wanted to get a better feeling for the man behind the image of Brigham Young. Although he spent winters here with one of his wives and no children for several years, it yielded few clues about his inner nature.

Perhaps what was missing was for me the biggest clue. Neither Carla nor I felt any spiritual uplift while at his house. Our guides were a sweet couple, obviously devoted Mormons, but even with their enthusiasm there was little I took away about "The Prophet." Perhaps since it is not my path to God I have no resonance with the man, but I had wanted to get a spiritual measure of this powerful man in Mormon history. He had a large library of books and was a voracious reader. He learned to read from his mother, had only 16 days of formal education but was instrumental in launching two universities that continue to educate today.

From St. George, Utah, we left the state, crossed the corner of Arizona and entered our sixth state, Nevada. Letting Ram be our guide, we drove south and came to the Valley of Fire State Park. We were charmed as we entered the campground, it had all the appearances of a movie set for the Flintstones and the town of Bedrock. Rounded red rocks in surprising shapes and thousands of little caves and delightful contours met us at every angle.

The next day we took a tour of the road leading up to the White Domes, we hiked through Rainbow Vista, and at the end of the road, we took the steep climb down to the Narrows at the White Domes. The Narrows are wide enough to let one person pass through at a time, with a winding path that would make a serpent's tail look straight, and cliffs rose straight up on either side beyond sight. The entire walk was most wonderful and was a demonstration of how far I have come in these past weeks; this walk would have been inconceivable just a week ago. Nevada has demonstrated that Utah has nothing on it in terms of beautiful canyons and unusual rock formations here at Valley of Fire.

Carla ready to enter the Zion Canyon Narrows.

Both at Snow Canyon and here at Valley of Fire, we have had little or no phone/internet connection. Tonight, we will drive 45 minutes each way to make a Skype call to the Victoria Center and I hope to be able to send this posting out at that same time. Know that you continue in our thoughts and prayers, and that this Pilgrimage North America continues to yield a wonderful prescription of extraordinary locations and purifying vibrations.

November 7

GOD AS OUR TOUR GUIDE

Camped at Valley of Fire: Looked as if we were dropped into the set of a Flintstones movie in the town of Bedrock.

I don't think there could ever be two polar opposites as extreme as my father and me when it comes to making travel plans. My mother and father traveled extensively all over the world, going on tours that were well planned in advance. I, on the other hand, have only one plan, what does God have in mind for me today?

When I asked my father where he was going on his next trip, I thought I might get a brief answer of what continent(s) they would be going to, what countries, and possibly some highlights of special sites they planned to see. Instead, I would get a ream of papers organized and stapled together with daily itineraries. Such details as what time they were to get up, when they would arrive for breakfast, and the minute they were to leave on the tour bus would come my way. Each and every fifteen minutes of the day was planned, and you better take care if you are the tour guide and there is any transgression in the timetable, for my father's famous temper could erupt at such inconvenient inconsistencies!

How his son travels is so different that you would think we came from distant planets. God is the tour guide, and He must make all arrangements as things unfold. Mother once said that when organizing an event, create a skeletal plan, and then let God fill in the details. And, if God wished to rearrange the skeleton, then let Him do so.

In leaving on this pilgrimage there were only the barest of skeletal plans. I have had some notion that we would circumambulate the North American Continent in a contrary, counter-clockwise direction (traditional pilgrimage circumambulations are clockwise). I knew we would begin with a tour of the Utah Canyons that are justifiably known for their tremendous beauty and grandeur. God prompted this pilgrimage for purposes fully known only to His all-knowing omniscience. I have some hints from Him, and He has revealed other parts of His plan as we have continued this journey, but it always makes it interesting to find deeper reasons as I assiduously follow His will.

What I find truly awe-inspiring is how He takes care of us with unfailing love and attention to detail. Some may call it coincidence or lucky breaks, but when time after time His total inner direction and outer answers to our needs are miraculously fulfilled, one must finally come to the conclusion that luck or coincidence simply does not suffice to explain how He perfectly takes care of us.

Last night we knew we would have to travel some miles to find a phone connection that would enable us to make a Skype call to the Victoria Group. Earlier in the day, we traveled to the only nearby town to scout out a strong signal and get a few things at the store. Even though the town sported a Community College we had zero connection for our phone service. While driving back there was one stretch of road that showed promise of 4G with three bars; it would be sufficient. Turns out, in the entire area we scouted, there was less than a quarter mile of road that had any phone connection, and there happened to be a reasonable gravel turnout where we could park by the side of the highway just where the signal was the strongest.

Later that night we drove to the same spot and found it now had only one bar strength, and that would definitely not be enough. However, since that was the only spot we had found any connection, we turned it over to God and continued to set up the tablet and tethered it to the extraordinary phone Chad provided for us. At the appointed time we made the call, and for nearly an hour we had perfect connection with that most wonderful group of souls in Victoria. When we finished, I looked at the phone connection and we had 4G at four bars; thank you Ram!

Today we decided to leave Valley of Fire Campground due to cold winds picking up; we headed for places unknown. Carla saw there was a well-rated campground on Lake Mead at Boulder Beach for only 10 dollars a night. When we arrived, we found a lovely corner campground spot with an unobstructed view of the deep blue waters of Lake Mead and a red mountainous backdrop; much warmer weather and no winds, thank you Ram!

So, you see, we don't do too badly with God as our tour guide. And although this trip can have all the appearances of a vacation or holiday, it varies significantly in that from stem to stern it has been dedicated to His service. I can tell you that in the last twenty-four hours He has inwardly worked me relentlessly, giving me a load to carry that is almost more than I think that I can bear. Of course, that is true, of myself I cannot carry the load He has given me; He must make that possible as He also makes such perfect arrangements for our travel and sees to every other detail in our lives. Living in perfect trust of following His will, and depending only on His abundant supply, I would have it no other way.

November 15

PILGRIMAGE'S TWISTS AND TURNS

Olympic Mountains and Puget Sound upon our return.

From our wonderful time on Skype with the Victoria Group onward my energy and health took a downturn. Mornings had lately been the lowest energy ebb, but now I was not picking up at all through the day. Also, the burning pain in my stomach persisted, and after two weeks it seemed a good idea to at least get the blood level checked again.

Sure enough, my hemoglobin count had dropped again to a six. Boulder City hospital transferred me to Valley Hospital in Las Vegas; Carla followed the ambulance in a rented car. Entering into the emergency entrance strapped to a gurney was like entering a movie set. I was lined up with another six new patients also on gurneys. There was noise and controlled chaos as I lay just inside the sliding doors.

Ram was present in the alcoholic-dementia man who was talking to no one in particular about events in the 1970s, an elderly woman calling out, "Help, help me," about every ten seconds, and nurses and doctors all busy going to and fro. Finally, I was taken to an adjoining room that felt to be kept at 60 degrees. I was attended by a nurse who was a double for my nephew Chad. An East Indian doctor came in and said he would be my primary doctor, talking very fast and laughing repeatedly, he came in and went out in about a minute. After many hours during which there was a loud fire alarm and strobe lights flashing for over five minutes while shifting in an uncomfortable gurney without knowing what would be done with me next, I was eventually taken to the Medical Intensive Care Unit (ICU) room at about midnight. There I was hooked up to five or six electrical monitors. I was poked repeatedly for blood and places to begin the infusion of fluids.

Many have commented on how spectacular the lights are at night in Las Vegas, however my only experience of lights while in Las Vegas were the many bouncing lights on monitors! That, and three walls and a ceiling of an ICU room. One nurse came in, an event that occurred about every half-hour throughout the night, and told me with a laugh that I had not checked into the Comfort Inn; I heartily agreed. That was also apparent from the lack of room service, as I was given nothing to eat or drink for 28 hours due to the anticipated endoscopy. With all seriousness though, I received excellent and friendly care while there.

God also gave me an opportunity to talk to the night nurse about the challenges of parenting, offering some thoughts she found helpful, and giving sympathy to another nurse who was dealing with a son who had diabetes, which softened her mood extremely. Truly, caregivers are often in need of care themselves.

With further treatment needed for a mass found in the duodenum it seemed the prudent thing was to return to home ground;

so, we have now arrived at Camano Island. These are some of the many twists and turns that have occurred in this pilgrimage.

God being the all-powerful controller has continued to plan for everything perfectly, however it may look on a human level. The prayer that comes back to me again and again is Mother's saying, "Lord, let this be fulfilled for the highest good of everyone concerned." Be it so.

November 19

PATIENCE AND PERSISTENCE

*Krishna Tells The Gita to Arjuna***

P art of the journey of this pilgrimage for us is the unexpected
need to learn to navigate through the medical/insurance
complex. Like all of life's undertakings, it requires a combination of patience and persistence.

Fortunately, I have had Carla as a partner in this endeavor. She
has pushed to get doors to open and uses me as the big hammer
backup when her efforts do not yield results. This began at the
end of last year in signing up for health insurance. Even though an
entire bureaucracy had been set up to get first time people to be
enrolled, bewilderment and frustration only seemed to build with
each interaction. However, at a time when Carla just wanted to
let it all go, some inner force in me kept insisting that we must

have health insurance; something neither one of us have had since leaving jobs that provided it.

With a few calls from the "big hammer" the doors of health-care slowly swung open and we were enrolled. Flash forward to October and the beginning of our need for health insurance made itself known. Even though we had a very large initial deductible, the specialist doctor in Moab assured us that we would easily exceed those amounts with the hospital stay.

I have to say, this modern system has literally saved my life. Without the blood transfusions and various procedures, it is no stretch to say I would not still be living very long without these interventions. I am very grateful for those who have dedicated a significant portion of their lives to learning the skills to care for individuals whose bodies have ceased to function properly.

With that being said, there are also gaps in our current system that could be bettered. One area was when we returned to Camano. I had not had a primary care physician (a PCP) due to the fact that I have not needed one in the 40 plus years since I had a family physician that my parents arranged. I had been to see a physician a total of three times in those 40 years, and two of those times had been walk-in clinics. The insurance wanted me to now have a PCP, but calls around would require two plus weeks to see someone; and my blood count had gone from 8.3 to a dangerous 5.1 in the previous two weeks. Two weeks was too long to wait to get in to see a physician.

So, Carla called in the big hammer, me. I called the 24-hour insurance nurse and told her it was recommended by the specialist doctor in Las Vegas that the best way to get in to see a doctor was to go to the hospital emergency room. The nurse was appalled a doctor said this, which he did, and I think dollar signs started to roll around in her head that the insurance would need to pay for such a visit. Suddenly she remembered they had a case management program; a case manager is an RN on the phone who was there to help you navigate the medical system.

With the very helpful case manager I had a doctor's appointment for the next morning with an internist, who in turn made an appointment with a surgeon for Friday, and a PCP appointment for the next Tuesday in nearby Stanwood. Suddenly things were moving and felt to be on a good track. The internist also called to the lab that was supposed to have my results on Monday or Tuesday. This was Wednesday, and she talked directly to the lab tech, something Carla had not been able to do with repeated calls. He explained the first "staining" tests came back negative, but he wanted to run another series of tests; they would have the results in the next day (today).

This persistence had paid off! But along with the persistence has been patience. Waiting for results of a test that can have very large implications can be trying. It is both in the persistence and the patience that our spiritual life can play such a large roll. Attunement with God brings strength of will to act, along with faith that doors will open according to His will. This attunement also gives us patience, for all is ultimately in His hands.

We learn to strike when He prompts us to strike, and to reside in Him in pure trust when there is nothing for us to take action upon. Like the wise blacksmith, he knows that to strike upon iron when it is not yet up to temperature is uselessly spent energy. When the iron glows the right color of red, then it is time to strike the iron to give it the shape wanted. So too, when listening to God, He prompts us to strike when it will do the maximum good. Anxiousness will have us flailing about uselessly, wearing ourselves out with what turns out to be destructive actions because we are not attuning ourselves to Him.

This great lesson in life presents itself to you in many guises. Through school, in families and work situations, and in all situations of life, you are given the opportunity of learning to attune and trust your life to the all-powerful Lord residing in your heart and soul. Recognize His prompting to act when you must, without being held back by fear or attachment. To learn this most basic of spiritual lessons is to become free, for the burden resides upon God's shoulders and He must devise what is to be done in any situation. What freedom there is in this loving, trusting, and intimate attunement with the Infinite Spirit within you.

November 22

HEALING MESSAGES

Garland placed in Anandamayi Ma's
Samadhi Temple, Kankhal, India.

On this beautiful Sunday morning I had the inner prompting to post a sampling of the beautiful messages sent to
Carla and me in the past weeks. Please feel the same
upliftment and spiritual power that I do when reading these
heartfelt messages. In addition to these writings that reflect such
wonderful souls in God, I have been reading from a book Mother
used to read from by Eva Bell Werber, *Quiet Talks with the Master.*
I also add this YouTube video of Yoganandaji and Ma sent to me
by Christopher.[12]

※   ※   ※

---

12   https://www.youtube.com/watch?v=Qo46Etdc9Ak

Health Update: We continue to wait for the biopsy results from Valley Hospital in Las Vegas. The last word we received was their initial tests were negative, but they continue to do additional "stain" tests. I have an appointment on Monday with a surgeon who specializes in the field of medicine that connects with my condition. If we have not heard before, the surgeon should be able to get an update on the long overdue biopsy results. I have felt and been sustained by your love and prayers. Pronams, David

MESSAGES

Dear David, we are just at Sri Ma's ashram at Kankhal for the samyan saptah, and got the news of the latest health situation. In the meantime I offered a garland (mainly marigolds) on your behalf, to be placed on Sri Ma's (Anandamayi Ma) Samadhi.

. . . have been a bit keyed up, since I got home. I went into the room in which I meditate to put some things away. I felt a strong pull toward my altar. I stood there, at God's direction, looked at the Masters and closed my eyes. I asked for guidance and a calm presence. What presented was you, in big form. I saw you surrounded by the Masters, then your tumor exploded into many pieces of light, which spread out. Then the vision changed to you sitting there in the center of the Masters, with light shooting from the crown chakra, much like fireworks. I could not break the gaze and remained as long as was requested. As I opened my eyes, the altar was somewhat different than I envisioned. I had envisioned you in the center, which you were, but in fact your picture is a bit off to the side, leaning against Lahiri Mahasya's picture. The Masters surround the both of you. I have attached the picture of you that I have on the altar. What struck me was how clear and pure you looked. What a vision to carry!

I am praying for God's best outcome for all that is occurring with your health. Surely, I have had much thought and caring, and am hoping for a speedy and full recovery for you, my Beloved Guru.

I want you to know that I see the Light of the Divine Mother flowing all around you and through you permeating every atom, every molecule of your entire being . . . vibrating, shining, radiating like a thousand suns. You shine like a beacon, blinding any darkness that could possibly come near you. In my mind's eye I can only see you right now, in this moment, as perfect, healthy, whole, and complete.

Last week I woke up early in the morning very much concerned about you. I wake up in bed early every morning with my mind fixed on God, and as I relayed these concerns to God, a simple and soothing answer came back very clearly, "David is full of light and full of peace." And then I didn't worry so much anymore. Although I am still concerned, I know you are always being taken care of in the best possible way.

You are always in our prayers. More so now. As you know very well Ram is busy doing miracles for His people like you. Your narration is a testimony to that. You are in good hands there.

A few days ago, I was feeling a resentment cropping up toward an imagined slight, and then, without effort, a thought of you filled me with love and upliftment and erased that thought with love. Every day such thoughts of You and Mother bring love to my heart and mind. Though in body you may for now be weak, but in Spirit you are strong. May your body be filled with healing light. Pronams in gratitude to you.

The other day I was chatting with Shree Ma (Anandamayi Ma) about David. She was right in front of me and smiled so lovingly. She then stood in front of David who was in a sitting position. She raised both her hands and placed them on the top of his head, immediately there was such a feeling of Pure Love, Softness, and Light pouring all over him: no idea how long it lasted. But, what a Blessing and Joy.

Carla, I can feel your Spiritual Strength and your willing answer to the call of this great Spiritual Challenge. You are truly answering that call. Well done!! Courage, bravery and so much love are present. God bless you, girl. We hold you both tenderly in our hearts and prayers.

We will be having a kirtan in your honor tomorrow. Please be available to receive our ardent transmission of love and prayer at the time. We trust that the healing process is already coming along nicely. The duodenum is vibrating with light. Old cells are sloughing off and new cells are being born. Victory to God.

Paramhansa Yogananda: "Father Thou art in me. I am well. The healing power of spirit is flowing through all the cells of my body. I am made of the one universal God substance."

Paramhansa Yogananda: "Heavenly Father, my body cells are made of light, my fleshly cells are made of Thee. They are perfect for Thou art perfect. They art health for Thou art health. They art spirit for Thou art spirit, they art immortal for Thou art life."

. . . "May the long time sun shine on you, all love surround you, may the pure light within you guide you all the way home."

May God and the Masters ever hold and keep you.

We can very well understand how Carla feels. We also pray for Beloved Papa's blessings on Carla for strength to handle everything. Once again all of us intensely pray for Beloved Papa's choicest blessings on you for speedy recovery and restoration to normal health.

Deepest love and best wishes for you, Carla, Judy, Rick and all there.

A lovely letter to all devotees and I am sure it will be very appreciated. Having also been the recipient of Healing Oms and prayers (as have many in our group) I too know their amazing power. One is so humbled by such love. I am grateful for the times sickness has enabled me to feel myself connected to all suffering souls in the world. The load you carry is universal, may the prayers and love you receive be sufficient to alleviate the burden and pain you bear. But as I write these words, I feel the Divine Mother so present with you; it is She in all these souls who prays for you and heals you; She holds you in Her arms. Om Om Om

Though the Almighty Lord of the Universe has blessed Reverend Davidji with a mindset to accept all situations stoically, still it disturbs us. Today on the occasion of our Beloved Swamiji's (Satchidanandaji) Jayanti, we fervently pray for HIS blessings on Reverend Davidji for a speedy recovery and restoration to normal health so that he may continue to guide the aspirants on the spiritual path.

My love calls out to you from every particle of my being and it is God too who prays so deeply for you through

me—for His perfect son. You are all radiance and bless-edness to me, ever in my heart and soul.

There is no end to Ram's adventures for us! The ways in which you are working with this one, provide excellent instruction for all. Blessings and love.

Hari Om! Hari Om! Hari Om!

Our hearts are with you in earnest prayer. What a painful mail it is.

May Papa, Mataji, and Swamiji help David, Carla and all of you at this hour, restore normalcy to our dear Davidji.

We are simply shocked again. Vimala has rushed to Homa Mandir to offer her prayers at the round. Shruti almost broke down. God alone is our refuge. David has taken so much of our karmas. Let us all do a chain RamNam – 10 minutes each person.

Lots of our prayers,

Chandra and all others join in the prayer.

My dear guru, I pray to God to heal you completely. Knowing all that has happened to you during your pilgrim-age health wise has checked me in feeling so sorry and sad about myself, and here you are having so much pain. My wishes and prayers are for you to gain all your health as you are so much needed in these times of life. Giving all my love to you, and not to forget our loving Carla. Thank you, my beloved guru. Om Sri Ram Jai Ram.

All our prayers are with you for David to recover completely and to live a normal life with all of us, without any pain or disease. As we all need that pure soul with us for our spiritual upliftment, I am sure that Papa will ensure a speedy recovery to complete normalcy.

Our prayers also for lots of strength to all of you there who are physically serving David.

We are thinking of you, surrounding you in light and meditating with all our might and main.

How extraordinary your cosmic journey, surveying heights and depths, inside and out! How my heart has wept, as you are taken through flames of unbearable suffering, witnessing His drama as a spectator beholds fields leveled and seeds ripening in the dark!

My heart beams you many rays of healing light during this time. May the outcome be the one that God is pleased with the most (and us too). May God answer our prayers to have you with us for a long time yet. Love to you both.

Prayers from our dear little ones.

November 26

A Keen Sense of Gratitude on This Thanksgiving Day

Happy Thanksgiving.**

Thanksgiving is a wonderful holiday, a day dedicated to feeling gratitude for all the good things we have received in life. One of the qualities I have noticed about being uplifted in pure Spirit—gratitude is always heightened. Everyone suffers to some degree in life, and our attitude about that suffering becomes a habit. Either you can focus on what is wrong to the exclusion of the blessings you have, or you can cultivate gratitude and count your blessings (instead of sheep as the Irving Berlin song goes).

This is a day set aside for counting our blessings and giving gratitude to God for what we have been given. In the early days, American citizens were asked to fast and pray if something had gone wrong, from natural disasters such as droughts, all the way to a lost battle in a war. And when things were good, it was to be celebrated with a feast of thanksgiving and prayer dedicated to the Creator.

Canada and the United States have different dates for the Thanksgiving holiday, but the spirit is the same. As I think of all the things I have to be thankful for, the list is very long. What stands first and foremost is that God and Guru plucked me out from the sea of darkness and ignorance, and through long purification, have made me know that, "I and my Father are one."

Other thoughts of blessings are for the many kindred spirits God has brought me into close contact with so that we may all go to God together (this brings a thrill to my heart). And this very early morning as I write this it is freezing outside, and a full moon is slowly sailing over the sky, creating a moon river on the Saratoga Straights; I am so grateful to have a warm home and a keen appreciation for the beauty that lies right outside the frosty windowpane.

I have been the recipient of so much love and ardent prayers, it humbles me to dust. I see the progress (perhaps more clearly than the individuals see in themselves) that so many aspirants are making in their realization of God; oh, my spirit can barely contain itself in seeing this progress! I also see the way many limit themselves in their growth of consciousness. But I know that the seed of yearning will not be denied, and though the outer shell of the seed may resist the power of growth, soon the limiting shell will burst wide open as tender shoots reach out to the light.

I am truly thankful for the lifesaving role that allopathic medicine has recently played in my life. I have my criticisms of modern medicine, but there is no doubt that blood transfusions and the promise of remarkable scans made of this body lead to effective treatment. My life has been saved by those who have dedicated so much of their lives to healing the sick.

These stand out to me as highlights of gratitude for all that has been given to me. I would only add that God has also given me service to perform in this world, and though this service may take its toll, I would have it no other way. It is such a great privilege to be His minister and serve Him in all forms as He directs me to do. To be His instrument brings about the greatest sense of fulfillment I have ever known. For this, I deeply give thanks.

Thank you my dear friends for sharing in this journey with me and adding your light of God. A powerful and pure stone of truth can create a ripple effect that changes all creation. May our journey be such a rock of truth that all creation must improve in order to accommodate that absolute force of truth and love it emanates.

Health Update: Things have moved at a remarkable speed in what can be a stodgy medical system. I have become a patient of Dr. S., a specialist on internal organs and glandular medicine. His medical assistant described him in this way: some doctors have good communication skills but are not the best technical doctors, and some are technically great but have a poor ability to relate to others; Dr. S. has both, and adding something rather impolitic, I would not work for any other doctor here! When we were at another clinic the nurse had done her externship with Dr. S. and began to spontaneously sing praises of him as well!

On Monday, when I first met the doctor, he spent over an hour with Carla and me and described my case as very complicated, like someone encountering a puzzle he was excited to unravel. He ordered another CAT scan that was done immediately after my appointment with him. He also ordered a PET scan; he said it would take at least a week to be approved by insurance, and they may deny it altogether, but he felt the test was necessary. With the invaluable help of our insurance case manager the approval came in two days time and I am scheduled for this test on Friday. My hemoglobin count has gone down slightly from a ten to a nine but remains out of the danger zone.

The good doctor called me on his day off, the day before Thanksgiving, and he left a long message saying that the second CAT scan showed I had a "telescoping intestine." He seemed to indicate this may be the real culprit in the blood loss. He also mentioned that he found no evidence of a lesion on my liver, as the previous scan had suggested; it was speculated that the lesion might indicate metastatic cancer. His overall tone was cautiously optimistic. I will seem him again next Wednesday.

The fact the doctor's medical assistant couldn't believe I saw the doctor so quickly (he had a cancellation and I was put into that timeslot), that I was approved at all for the PET scan and in such record time, that I had a CAT scan scheduled an hour after my first doctor's appointment, all indicate a higher power at work. The speed of my treatment continues to amaze the very people who work in this field. I know your continued prayers help clear the way from obstacles that may otherwise greatly delay or stymie the process. The one indecipherable aspect that runs contrary to this smooth flow of events is that my biopsy report from Las Vegas is still *missing in action* (Perhaps lending credence to the saying that what happens in Las Vegas stays in Las Vegas!). Dr. S. said that the most recent scans may render those results moot. A bit of a mystery there, but I am sure he will further explain next Wednesday.

An additional observation and point of gratitude: Carla has been a dharmic warrior throughout this process: asking questions, filling out endless forms, making multiple daily phone calls—keeping the machinery moving forward at as high a speed as possible. When the doctor talked about ordering the PET scan, Carla's adamant reply, Yes! came out before the doctor had finished his sentence.

It is an unfortunate state of affairs that oftentimes it is the squeaky wheel that gets attention, and Carla has brooked no opposition in getting treatment for this body. And fortunately, the medical practitioners have always agreed; avoiding large transfusions of blood is highly desirable and has been a goal of theirs as well, which means things must happen in a timely way or it is likely I will need new blood in not too long a time.

In the big picture, all is surrendered to the will of God and my continuing prayer is that His will be fulfilled for the highest good of all. So, my dear ones, may you have a blessed Thanksgiving and may the Grace of God, Christ, Gurus ever be upon you and fill you with inspiration and a keen sense of gratitude.

November 29

FREEDOM IN THE DIVINE PRESENCE

Jesus in the Cosmos.

Jnana translates as discrimination: "This is not of God and this is of God, the highest Light and Truth." Jnana helps to clear us from attachment by our dis-identifying with those things that are not of God, and immersing ourselves into those things that are of God. There are many categories of attachment that ensnare the mind, but the body-mind relationship is certainly one of the most powerful.

Identification with the body means that when our body feels pleasure or pain we have no separation between those sensations and who we are. We are seduced from an early age by pleasure. We like the feeling of pleasure and become totally consumed by wanting more and more and thus creating attachment. Of course, pain is also present when living in a body, and our attachment to pain even further roots us in the body. We come to forget that in Spirit we are free of attachment to either pleasure or pain, because we have bliss which has no opposite.

Obviously if we live in a body, we will be subject to pleasure and pain, but the key is to have superior bliss, and in this way, we detach from pure body identification. Desire for pleasure and the fear of pain cements our identification with the body, so both must be given up. It is interesting how attachment to pain through fear is so powerful. You would think that giving up attachment to pain would be easy, as it is not something wanted, yet the fear of pain is a powerful magnet that draws the mind and makes it very attached to the body.

An important turning point in this regard came for me when I was at Anandashram. I was quite sick for several weeks running a very high fever and I had tremendous pain in the body. I was inwardly talking to Papa saying, "Papa, you say that pain and bliss are the same, right now I only feel pain; you **must** show me how pain and bliss are the same." Suddenly I was lifted up in a vision in which I saw Papa opposite to me. He had a toothless smile and took my hands, we started to dance around and around in a circle; he was laughing and I was filled with bliss. I was still aware that my body was in pain, but I was even more aware of being filled with bliss. Then I "saw" that the same life-force that flowed to the brain as pain signals was also flowing into the brain as bliss. On that level pain and bliss were the same!

This started a thought process that continued over time in which anytime the body had pain, I would go to the substratum of seeing that it was God's life-force that was carrying the pain signals to my brain. Immediately upon seeing this, the vast majority of pain would transmute itself into pure life-energy and bliss; leaving some pain signal but much reduced. I also learned that when we focus on pain as an absolute and fear becomes the driver, it intensifies pain tremendously.

Losing fear of pain, seeing the underlying life-force as coming from God behind the pain signals, and then feeling God's Presence in the form of bliss have a tremendously palliative effect in suffering. Not only can it ease suffering in itself, it also opens intuition so that the Divine Force may be free to effect a cure.

Recently, I have written much about the condition of this body giving you updates on what the medical care providers have been saying. However, it is important to note that more important than what doctors and nurses say, what does God say? More importantly than what symptoms this body displays, what is the all-powerful life-force doing in and around the body? And more important than what pain or discomfort this body may be in at any particular time, what bliss is flowing through my being? What I can tell you is that God is fully present and accounted for. His bliss is even now flowing through my spine and brain and through all the cells of my body. Truly there is nothing but He, even when there is weakness, pain, or discomfort, it is all He! Let not this talk of the body and medical procedures (which I find interesting) make you forget there is something far greater going on daily.

"Why then," you may ask, "is there a physical problem when God is present?" There are many times when God's Presence can and does manifest as complete physical healing. However, there are a variety of causes that manifest as physical problems, and there are times when God will use His physical instruments to fulfill His higher will. Thus, there is no contradiction in His perfection and in His use of a physical body to fulfill a necessary karma, or to bring about desirable outcomes on this earth (As Jesus said, "This sickness will not end in death but is for the glory of God" John 11:4).

Meditate deeply upon this important concept of jnana: discriminating between what is of God and what is not of God. Learn to go beyond the things of the body and this world; know that God is the supreme Presence that assuages all pain and ignorance and makes us know we are one with the Omniscient Lord. It is in this knowledge that we will find freedom and bliss in the Divine Presence.

December 7

BE BORN ANEW

Paramhansa Yogananda.**

A devotee recently said that she planned to spend Christmas Eve and morning alone, deeply meditating instead of rushing about to far-flung family. She had a glow as she spoke of this coming event.

While many may not be in a position to take this time away from the many events scheduled during these holidays, I would very much encourage you to plan time for your spiritual Christmas, as well as your social Christmas. If the holidays are only for eating and drinking and making merry, then where is the time for celebrating the birth of Christ?

Sri Yoganandaji used to take the day before Christmas for a six-hour meditation at Mount Washington. Oftentimes he would have visions of Jesus during this time and feel deep communion with him. Then on Christmas day he would have a social Christmas with food and the exchanging of gifts. He was balanced in all ways.

This is a powerful time of year and we can live it in such a way that wears us out through activity, or we can feel melancholy and blue, or we can live it in balance; celebrating the birth of Christ Consciousness within and enjoying a social Christmas as well. We can drink deeply from the well of Bliss within, and then share that Divine Light with all the world. How much more do we have to share with this world when we have contacted God first!

Even though I may not be able to be with you in body for these Christmas celebrations, I will definitely be with you in Spirit. I would remind you that the breadth and depth of Christ Consciousness cannot be fully fathomed by the human mind; so there is always more for us to experience, learn, and be transformed by as we dive deeper and soar higher in this mighty venture of knowing God.

Do not let your mind limit you to the possibilities of what you may be as you grow in Christ Consciousness. You are a child of the Infinite, and as such you are made in His likeness and image. This season symbolizes the birth of this supreme Consciousness into the world and in you. Be sure to capture its sacred significance as it approaches and receive God's great gift for you—to be born anew in Christ Consciousness.

Health Note: The most recent news has come from the long-awaited results of the Las Vegas biopsy. Dr. S. said it surprised him but the tumor showed signs of being melanoma. When I said

I thought of that as skin cancer he said yes, it starts on the skin, but can migrate to different parts of the body. He thought I must have had the cells on the skin but my immune system successfully fought it off. Then some of the cells floated through the blood system and started growing in the stomach. There are times when the immune system does not recognize that these cells do not belong and the tumor is left to grow. They will take further samples during the operation but he feels confident it will confirm this diagnosis, as it fits all the facts known so far. In aftercare I would receive immunotherapy; boosting the immune system so that the immune system recognizes and destroys any future growth of these melanoma cells. They will also use some of my cells for a research project to develop a vaccine for others. My hemoglobin count has dropped more, but is not at the point of needing transfusions. The doctor has ordered intravenous iron to be injected early this week before the operation, which is still scheduled for December 10th at 10 a.m.

Additional Note: There are a large number of recent emails stating I have appeared in many dreams. In all cases it has been assuring to the dreamer that all is well, with everything proceeding toward positive results. As always, it is wonderful to hear from you.

December 9

BLESSINGS OF GOD, GURUS AND YOU

I pronam to you: Sunset on the
shores of the Arabian Sea, India.

I thank you all for your great love and prayers over these last months. I feel like I am in good hands for this surgery tomorrow. I was in for a maximum iron infusion last evening. The attending nurse had worked at the University Hospital for many years with some top surgeons there. For the last couple of years, she has been at Providence. She said if there was anyone she would want as a surgeon, it would be my surgeon.

I think I have the easiest "job" tomorrow, that is, to show up for the surgery. Others will be working hard, and some may have worries, but I will be fast asleep!

I do not know what recovery will look like afterwards, but when I can I will let you know how I am doing. I am sure that in between time Carla and Cate will send out notices on my current status. For now, I am doing well, the body is very tired and has its ways of showing its displeasure, but I feel the blessings of God, Gurus and you.

December 22

WINTER SOLSTICE SOARING

View of Himalayas from Dhaulchina (Cheena), India.

Each year the earth's rotation around the sun brings the northern hemisphere to its furthest distance from the solar center, the winter solstice. It is the darkest time of year and symbolically it is the death of the calendar year. Since ancient times there has been a connection with the change of seasons, the movement of the stars, and changes in consciousness.

When I first became aware of awakening to higher consciousness, I did not need an astrologer to tell me that the winter solstice had powerful influences, for I was fully cognizant that each year it would take me into a deep experience. The annual buildup to the solstice was always a powerful and difficult time for me. There are many people who talk of having holiday blues, and while there are many human reasons for this, there are also many who are consciously or unconsciously experiencing the influence of the winter solstice.

A great feeling of psychic pressure and isolation would descend on me weeks before the solstice. Since my late teens, I was aware through pre-natal memories and Grace that there was something more to life than simple human existence. I did not have a name for this something more, it might be God, but if it was, it was different than a vague or philosophical notion of God, it had to do with something deeply personal, yet beyond my personhood; I had an incredibly strong drive and need to know what that something was. Each year the build-up to Christmas, and more explicitly to the solstice, was like entering into the threshing floor where the wheat is beaten in order to release the grain of realization from the chaff of ignorance.

There is an important difference between a crisis that involves the ego only and a spiritual crisis. The ego looks exclusively to itself in such a crisis, becoming more self-involved by feeling sorry for itself and looking to blame others or feeling shame at its own existence. In a spiritual crisis, the self looks beyond the ego to find answers; it expands rather than contracts. My spiritual crisis of the solstice would, just as predictably and mysteriously, lift with the apex of the solstice; then I would feel its uplifting power.

The chick that is still surrounded by the shell of the egg begins to peck at the shell, knowing somehow that the answer to a larger world lies outside of the shell. With increasing vigor, it pecks and pecks at the limiting shell to find release. If some outside force broke the shell apart prematurely the chick would not develop properly, and it would be prone to sickness and death. Likewise, there is something in the struggle to know God by pecking apart the shell of ignorance that is necessary for the development of the individual—otherwise, the realized Self would not fully develop.

Realization brings a new way of looking at life-experiences. The pain and difficulties of the past are still remembered; however, there is now a known purpose behind every blow taken in life, and this makes all the difference. When we come to know there is an exact and ennobling reason for everything that happens, then spiritual suffering is resolved—the largest portion of suffering in the world. I now see how each painful build-up to the solstice down through the years was awakening a greater inner resolve to know God.

During this past year the build-up to the solstice "crisis" has been of a physical nature. This body went through three hospitalizations culminating in the removal of three tumors and the removal of three sections of the small intestine. This morning as this solstice arrives, I have felt a definite inward release from the body's crisis. It began this a.m. with an experience with Mother and Father Hamilton, replaying many scenes of their early spiritual life together through my inner vision. Then came an infusion of spiritual power flowing into this body; this was followed by an inspiration to write to you about the nature of the winter solstice. Now a surge of bubbling blissful joy is flooding my being and radiating out. Without pre-awareness on my part, the body and spirit continue to replicate the pattern of the winter solstice cycle with the precision of a cosmic clock. Do we not live in a marvelous and wonder-filled universe?

I have often thought we missed the timing of the birth of Christ by a few days—what should have been the winter solstice. There is a definite uplifting spiritual current that comes at this time. I am reminded of my stay at a small ashram established by Anandamayi Ma in the Himalayas at Dhaulchina. Watching from the porch of the small dharmashala at the ashram perched on a plateau hundreds of feet above a valley floor below, we could see giant eagles launch themselves from nearby tree branches with barely a flap of their wings and then soar upon the updrafts. Six-foot wings made them soar without effort.

Taking full advantage of this change at the winter solstice, stretch your wings and feel the solstice's uplifting currents and fly with "wings as eagles" (Isaiah 40:31).

December 25

THE LIGHT EVER SHINING

The Virgin with Angel, painting by
William-Adolphe Bouguereau, 1900.**

This Christmas morning the full moon shines above as a beacon of light to all the darkened world below. This reminds
me that the Christ-child was born into this world to bring
Light and illumine all creation, for all those who would receive
the Light.

Avatars (the descent of Divinity into flesh) come to this world
to help awaken it to the fact that all creation is of Divine origin.

The world and those identified with it lose all relationship with their innate Divinity, and thus suffer and create further suffering for others. God, a respecter of humanity's free will, beckons all to rediscover the truth of their true nature. However, humankind is stubborn and stiff-necked in their adherence to being bound in their ignorance.

Therefore, God sends examples of fully realized Beings, avatars of immense spiritual realization and strength. These divinely realized Beings are not meant to be set up as idols and worshiped from a distance; rather, they come to awaken the same Divine nature in each individual that the avatar is awakened to within him or herself. It is our ignorance that says, "Divinity resides in that one only." This ignorance acts in opposition to the very reason why an avatar takes incarnation. To embrace and become fully awakened to one's own Divine nature fulfills the purpose of a Divine Incarnation.

To "receive" Jesus Christ is more than to proclaim faith in his Divinity, it means to realize through experience your same Divinity. It means you have looked within and you have seen the Divine Light shining as a star; you have been inspired by three wisdom kings to surrender the gold of the world, the bitterness of the world, and even your joy, and worship at the feet of the Christ-Light being born within you. It is to protect that Light from the vain jealousy and hatred of King Herod, seething within and seeking to destroy the Light. It is to love and nurture that Christ-Child-Light at every turn, to never deny it, or side with the forces of this world in their desire to suppress that same Light. To receive the Christ means that you experience the whole story within you.

So, on this precious Christmas morning, let us sense the sacred meaning embedded in these wonderful stories and images. Let us follow that star by going deeper into a meditative state in which we are illumined within by the Christ Light. Let us hear the angelic music of Spirit singing the song of Bliss and Joy that is within and everywhere about us and manifests as universal love and service. These are not just stories of another time and place, this is your journey, discovering who and what you truly are. It really is, as is said, "The Greatest Story Ever Told!"

It is in this Spirit that I write to you this morning, and it is my keen desire that you should know the truth of it. Not simply because I have said so, or that great realized Beings have told you so, but because you were inspired to seek this truth out within the laboratory of your own Being.

Please accept this as my Christmas Card to you, this year I simply have not been able to send out my usual Christmas Cards. We have received so many beautiful cards, and with each card I receive the love and good wishes sent with each of them. One card came from Dianne D. had this wonderful quote from C.S. Lewis that says so much: "The Son of God became a man to enable men to become Sons of God."

Have a joy-filled Christmas.

December 31

AWAKENED LIFE-FORCE

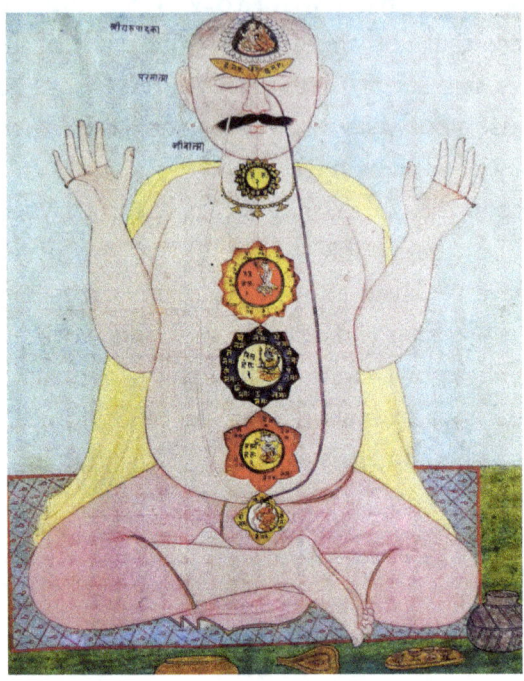

The Chakras of the Subtle Body

It has been interesting to observe the role of life-force during the past several months. With low blood counts for months before I went into the hospital, I relied upon life-energy coming in at the medulla oblongata and along the spine to fulfill what I was directed to do through this body. Even though it was a struggle, I was able to do all that God had asked me to do due to this vital energy that is independent of bio-chemical processes.

With the operation I had, and the recovery time immediately after, the role of life-energy was consumed with sustaining the body and enacting its healing. As I was healing, I continued to feel that life-force in the spine, and this added force made recovery go smoothly. Both doctors and nurses as well as visitors all commented on how well I looked; recovery was going extraordinarily well due to the role of life-force. Prayers from many, even from great distances, added enormously to the life-energy and its healing power.

Physical science has yet to recognize the role of life-force that is independent of, and superior to, biochemistry. It is evident that even though we all inhabit human bodies, we eat food and breathe oxygen, yet there are vast differences in the life-force we exhibit. It can run the gambit of extraordinary physical health and vitality, emotional range, mental liveliness, all the way to spiritual illumination. Physical science can explain part of why individuals have these differences, but it cannot explain it all.

As my body's recovery has continued, life-force (what in yoga is called prana) has been made available for other uses. As recovery proceeded, it was as if I was "waking up" to other areas of life. I could now envision our coming together for a Christmas/New Years' Service; the idea of doing more writing, being able to focus on Mother's Work, and opening myself to the "next phase" of my life's work all came alive for me.

There is no doubt that for full functioning in this world, the body needs to be an instrument that is in working order through biochemical processes; in this physical science has made tremendous progress. Like a vehicle, you are not going to get far if the car is mechanically unsound, and like with a computer, you are not going to be able to surf the web or use it to write if a virus is destroying it. However, even if the vehicle and the computer are functioning perfectly, they will simply remain inert without a human being operating them. Even so, a human body may have nothing physically wrong with it, but without a soul and spirit guiding the life-energy flowing through it, it will have no meaning and will not really come to life.

Here is the great discovery in ancient times by yogis: we can consciously access greater life-force by intelligent means. This allowed yogis to exist without oxygen for long periods of time, and to either heat or cool the body to counter temperature extremes. Life-energy is also a healing force and can be used to heal one's own body or to produce healing for others. As it comes to light in Western science, the discovery of life-force will be one of the great "new discoveries" of all time.

As an intelligent force, prana does not just respond to your conscious use of it, but also it will guide you. In this regard we may distinguish between two different forms of life-force. In the first case life-force guides natural processes, the growth of plants, movement of planets, and the health of human beings among billions of other functions in nature. There is also Prana we spell with a capital P. This higher, transcendent Prana is Divine Intelligence attuned to a much higher frequency of thought and energy than nature's prana.

We know this Prana through the awakened faculties in the spine and brain; at this time these faculties are usually dormant in human beings. Guidance gained through intuitive perception of higher consciousness is of a much greater order; it is an expression of Divine Will. Through merging human will with Divine Will, Prana forms the basis for the next stage of evolution. This is referred to as the transformation of the human into the Divine.

As we enter into this New Year, become conscious of prana life-energy coursing through your body as a tingling, electrical force that is necessary for all your body functions. Then stretch your subtle senses to feel that same vital force in nature, giving life and consciousness to water, trees, and animals. Through deep meditation, awaken awareness in your cerebrospinal system to Pranic Life-Force, the life-giving, blissful, and all-knowing Consciousness that has the capacity to lift you up into your oneness with God. Be a pioneer in this greatest of discoveries today and bring in the New Year with the promise of a much greater life! Have a blissful and prosperous New Year.

Conclusion

AFFIRMATION

I am a Loving Child of God

I am a loving child of God; Rich ideas from God are now pouring into my consciousness,

God gives me dominion over fear, hate, weakness, poverty,

And in harmony,

I am continually protected by God's love.

Disturbances cannot annoy me, because I abide in God's presence.

Through the help of God, I am master of my emotions.

No disappointment can disturb or discourage me.[13]

—YOGACHARYA DAVID

OM TAT SAT AUM

---

13   *Silence: Entering the Cosmic Sea of Consciousness* (p. 272).

Mount Temple, Alberta, Canada, painting by Dennis Brown.

References

Kondo, Marie. (2017). *The Life-Changing Magic of Tidying Up.* New York: Ten Speed Press.

Paramhansa Yogananda. (1982). *The Science of Religion.* Los Angeles: Self-Realization Fellowship.

Paramhansa Yogananda. (2013). *Demystifying Patanjali.* Los Angeles: Crystal Clarity Publishers.

Paramhansa Yogananda. (1946). *Autobiography of a Yogi.* New York: The Philosophical Library.

Hickenbottom, Yogacharya David. (2022). *Silence: Entering the Cosmic Sea of Consciousness.* Camano Island, WA.: The Cross and The Lotus Publishing.

Weber, Eva, Bell. (1936). *Quiet Talks with the Master.* New York: Devorss & Company.

Film References

Jesus of Nazareth. (1972). ITC Entertainment, RAI. Directed by Franco Zeffirelli.

An Honest Liar. (2014). Left Turn Films, Pure Mutt Productions and Part2 Filmworks. Directed by Justin Weinstein and Tyler Measom.

Bible References

King James Bible Online: https//www.kingjamesbibleonline.org

Website References

Mother Hamilton's quote reference: The Cross and The Lotus Publishing: www.crossandlotus.com

Yogacharya David's original discourse reference:
www.crossandlotus.com

Anandashram reference: www.anandashram.org

Image Attribution

With the exception of those listed below, all images are used courtesy of the David and Carla Hickenbottom portfolio. Photos were taken by David and Carla Hickenbottom or gifted with permission by friends, family, and devotees. Attribution for images from these sources has not been included here. Images of devotees or written submissions from devotees are all included after receiving consent for publication in this book series.

Images listed are available for free use in public domain, under Creative Commons licensing, or licensed from other sources as noted.

January 01. Paramhansa Yogananda, picture commonly known as "The Last Smile" by Arthur Say, 1952. Public domain.

February 07. *Lakshmi,* by Raja Ravi Varma (1848–1906). First published c. 1910. Commons.wikimedia.org. Public domain.

February 12. *Albert Einstein,* photographed by Orren Jack Turner, 1947. Commons.wikimedia.org. Public domain.

March 20. *Swami Sri Yukteswar,* c. 1920. *Autobiography of a Yogi,* page 109. (1946 Edition). Commons.wikimedia.org. Public domain.

March 27. Painting known as *Christ at 33,* by Heinrich Hofmann, extracted from his original work *Christ and the Rich Young Ruler,* 1889. Commons.wikimedia.org. Public domain.

April 03. *Abel Y Cain,* by LG UltraLink is licensed under Creative Commons CC-BY 3.0. Commons.wikimedia.org

April 06. *Resurrection of Jesus Christ,* by Keith Lance on iStockphoto.com. License purchased.

April 25. *Bhaktha Hanuman,* by Ravi Varma Press, 1930. Commons.wikimedia.org. Public domain.

April 28. *Murti of Dhanvantari,* at Ayurveda Expo, Bangalore by HPNadig is licensed under Creative Commons CC-BY-SA 3.0. Commons.wikimedia.org

May 01. Paramhansa Yogananda, cover portrait from *Autobiography of a Yogi.* (1946 Edition). Commons.wikimedia.org. Public domain.

May 05. *The Star of The Hero,* by Nicholas Roerich, 1936. Wikiart. org. Public domain.

May 15. *Released,* by Psychoshadowmaker on Dreamstime.com. License purchased.

May 19. *Jesus Casting out the Money Changers at the Temple,* by Carl Bloch, 1874. Wikiart.org. Public domain.

June 12. Master Mahasaya. Also: Mahendranath Gupta. *Autobiography of a Yogi,* p. 79 (1946 edition). Commons.wikimedia.org. Public domain.

June 17. *Hand-made Kris,* Bahasa, Indonesia by Sadhi Irawan is licensed under Creative Commons CC-BY-SA 4.0. Commons. wikimedia.org. Edited by The Cross and The Lotus Publishing.

July 04. *Statue of Liberty with Fireworks,* by Warren Rosenburg on Dreamstime.com. License purchased.

July 18. *Ganesha Writing the Mahabharata.* Unknown artist. Indianetzone.com. Public domain.

July 28. *The Incredulity of Saint Thomas,* by Caravaggio, c. 1602. Wikiart.org. Public domain.

November 19. *Krishna Tells (The) Gita to Arjuna,* by Mahavir Prasad Mishra. Mahabharata: Tej Kumar Book Depot. Commons.wikimedia.org. Public domain.

November 26. *Happy Thanksgiving Day in Wood Type,* by Marek Uliasz on Dreamstime.com. License purchased.

December 25. *The Virgin with Angels* or *The Queen of the Angels (Regina Angelorum),* by William-Adolphe Bouguereau, 1900. Commons.wikimedia.org. Public domain.

December 31. *The Chakras of the Subtle Body,* Unknown artist, c. 1820. Public domain.

Conclusion: *Mount Temple,* Alberta, Canada. Painting by Dennis Brown, with permission.

Acknowledgments

Yogacharya David has a unique ability to share spiritual teachings and soul-enhancing reflections in a most accessible manner—he can reach us in our day-to-day ways of being as we strive to live a purposeful life. He guides us, and, even as he laughs at himself, he still seriously advocates for a wake-up process.

It is a privilege to form what we call Team-David, a dedicated team of aspirants who willingly devote time and expertise to ensuring that Yogacharya David's legacy of teachings reaches those who long for a deeper, broader, disciplined-yet-freeing approach to life's journey.

Carla Hickenbottom, David's wife and senior disciple, has been a major support throughout the preparation and publication process. Her loving oversight and her diligence as director of The Cross and The Lotus Publishing support us each step of the way.

Rebecca Harvey has been a major ongoing link to data collection and historical document searches. She seems to know just where to find more information on most everything we need. Her keen eye also provides an astute read that catches the forever-escaping grammatical challenges. Mira Lutz, our other Team-David member for the Discourses, has an excellent knowledge of grammar. It is a gift of Grace to have such a fine team working to prepare and publish Yogacharya David's series of six Discourse volumes.

Our team also includes my editor, Zia Cole, for all of the Discourse volumes—our gratitude to her for her astute eye and professional expertise.

Jan Westendorp of Kato Design and Photo brings her artistic and professional book-design expertise forward when working on our manuscripts. She provides us with elegant page layouts and image-refinement support, and in so many other ways, she has helped us create a beautiful series of six volumes.

Team-David feels that Yogacharya David would be delighted to know that his unique writings and teachings are available in book form for all who seek a deeper, sacred understanding of the human condition.

About the Author

Yogacharya David Hickenbottom (1954–2019) met his guru Yogacharya Mother Hamilton, a disciple of Paramhansa Yogananda, when he was a youth of 20. Yogacharya David became a Reverend in 1984, and Mother Hamilton bestowed the Yogacharya title to David in 1989.

The great Kriya Yoga lineage of India that came through Jesus, Babaji, Lahiri Mahasaya, and Sri Yukteswar to Yogananda, and then to Mother Hamilton, provides pathways to: an appreciation of, and a faith in, the everyday sacred, an understanding of higher dimensional wisdom, an integral intuitive knowing of spiritual truths, and the vibratory realms that permeate all that is, was, and will be.

Yogacharya David says: "An inner pain brought me to the path most unwillingly, and this inner pain kept me on the path. I put my shoulder to the wheel." He faced the crux of the spiritual dilemma—how to shift from the ego-driven lower or smaller human nature to a larger and luminous existence, intuitively attuned to our deeper and broader—vast—spiritual nature, thereby discovering the Living Truth. With this intense striving for Truth and Bliss, and with his Guru's Grace, David was carried through many years of Mystical Crucifixion spiritual experiences. His year in silence (2000–2001) established an inner state of stillness that never left him—and finally led him to his full Self-realization.

ALSO BY YOGACHARYA DAVID

2013–2019 Discourses Series:

- *Discourses—Volume One: 2013–14: Living a Spiritually Rich Life*

- *Discourses—Volume Two: 2015: Re-Union of Soul and Spirit*

- *Discourses—Volume Three: 2016: A True New Birth*

- *Discourses—Volume Four: 2017: Gateway to the Infinite*

- *Discourses—Volume Five: 2018: Standing on the Threshold of Eternity*

- *Discourses—Volume Six: 2019: Writing in the Book of Life*

Hickenbottom, Yogacharya David. (2022). *Touching the Supreme Spirit.* Infinite Calendar. Camano Island, WA.: The Cross and The Lotus Publishing.

Hickenbottom, Yogacharya David. (2022). *Silence: Entering the Cosmic Sea of Consciousness.* Camano Island, WA.: The Cross and The Lotus Publishing.

Hickenbottom, Yogacharya David. (2022). *Notes to Sadhakas.* Camano Island, WA.: The Cross and The Lotus Publishing.

Hickenbottom, Yogacharya David. (2021). *Climbing the Sacred Mountain: Poems and Prayers of a Western Yogi.* Camano Island, WA.: The Cross and The Lotus Publishing.

Hickenbottom, Yogacharya David. (2019). *My Spiritual India.* Camano Island, WA.: The Cross and The Lotus Publishing.